MAKE MONEY ON YOUTUBE

How to Create and Grow Your YouTube Channel, Gain Millions of Subscribers, Earn Passive Income and Make Money Online Fast While Working From Home

By
James Ericson

that are mentioned are done without written consent and can in no way be considered an endorsement from the trademark holder.

TABLE OF CONTENTS

Introduction 1

Chapter 1 *What Is Youtube* 2

Chapter 2 *Making Your Channel* 8

Chapter 3 *Finding Your Voice* 20

Chapter 4 *Growing* 28

Chapter 5 *Leveraging Other Social Media* 41

Chapter 6 *Guide To Collaboration* 51

Chapter 7 *Money* 59

Chapter 8 *Becoming A Youtube Partner* 65

Chapter 9 *Affiliate Marketing* 73

Chapter 10 *Selling* 83

Chapter 11 *Fan Funding* 90

Chapter 12 *Self* 98

Conclusion 105

Description 106

INTRODUCTION

Congratulations on purchasing *Make Money On YouTube* and thank you for doing so.

The following chapters will discuss how you can turn YouTube in a career for yourself. Not just a career, but a fruitful one, one that will keep your head above the water for years to come.

YouTube has gone from a simple video sharing platform to a huge money machine for many different people, and you can totally be one of them. In this book, I'm not just going to outline the trick to making your video platform work, I'm going to make a point of including how exactly you can make money.

There are many different ways to make money on YouTube, to the point where there's no book that covers each and every way. But this book will give you a great look into it, and step by step instructions on how to make the most of each of them. You could even follow every single one on this book, although I'd recommend you never do more than one at a time before you master the next.

Making money with YouTube is the perfect way to take control of your career and livelihood, you're able to talk about the things you love and enjoy. Who could ask for a better job, spending all your day talking about the things you love?

There are plenty of books on this subject on the market, thanks again for choosing this one! Every effort was made to ensure it is full of as much useful information as possible, please enjoy!

CHAPTER 1
What Is Youtube

YouTube is one of the most popular websites in the world. You'd be hard pressed to find somebody who has never watched a YouTube video, mostly because it's everywhere. It's people's go to platform for when they want to post a video, whether it's something silly they want to send their friends or something full of information that they want to send out to the world. It's the number one place to go when you want video content, good or bad. As of 2019, it has nearly two billion monthly users, and that's not even counting all of the people who watch the site without an account. YouTube went from a tiny startup to an everyday part of our lives, similar to many other social media out there such as Facebook or Instagram.

YouTube started in 2005 when creators Chad Hurley, Steve Chen, and Jawed Karim all worked at PayPal, which at the time was another internet startup. Following the eBay buyout of PayPal, the three men used their bonuses that were received by it. There are rumors that the site initially started off as a dating website idea. This idea was scrapped after three separate occasions occurred where a video website would be useful: the first being that Karim was unable to find footage of the infamous Janet Jackson's Super Bowl wardrobe malfunction, the second that Hurley and Chen couldn't send footage of a dinner party, thanks to email's miniscule attachment limits at the time, and the third being a devastating tsunami that occurred on the Indian Ocean.

So, February 14th, Valentine's Day of 2005, they registered the website YouTube.com. The first ever YouTube video was uploaded several months later, April 23rd, 2015. It's a home video of Karim at the San Diego Zoo, titled Me At The Zoo. It's still online to this day. It's legitimately just a 19 second clip of Karim standing in front of the elephant pen and talking about their trunks.

It didn't take long before YouTube caught the eye of the internet, and people began flocking to the site. It gathered so much attention that Google eventually started investigating. They offered Chen, Hurley, and Karim $1.65 billion dollars, which they accepted. By May of 2010, the site was getting more than 2 billion views every single day, and by March of 2013, they were getting 1 billion monthly active users.

These numbers just kept growing. In 2019, the site has nearly 2 billion logged in monthly users and is now considered an essential part of our entertainment. 6 out of 10 people would rather watch online video over TV, and it's the number one entertainment service for millennials and generation Z. It's the world's second largest search engine, only out taken by its adopted father, Google, and is the third most visited website on the internet. Every day, more than 1 billion hours of content is watched.

But, it's not just the numbers that are so incredible about YouTube. YouTube was the start of the influencer culture. For those who don't know, influencers are people online, who post pictures, videos, and more to a large online following. The majority of beginner online influencers, such as PewDiePie, Shane Dawson, Tyler Oakley, Jenna Marbles, and Grace Helbig, starting posting just for fun, or to share silly videos with their friends. Before long, they had amassed online followings, and companies, and YouTube sat up and started to take notice. As time went on, more and more people started following and enjoying these creator's content. Many of the users had migrated over from Myspace, having had a ton of friends on that platform as well.

So, Google, who had begun running ads on the platform soon after it was bought, began offering these content creators a slice of the ad revenue. This was done to encourage YouTubers to not only make good content, but to make a lot of it, and to make it quickly. YouTube saw the value in these people and saw that they would bring a lot of people to the platform, rather than the person building their own website. And so it went, more and more people signed on to become YouTubers.

Many of them are household names now. It's launched the careers of many Hollywood stars, artists, makeup artists, musicians, athletes, and even comedians. Names include Jeffree Star, who now runs a huge makeup brand worth $75 million on top of a YouTube channel, Justin Bieber, who was discovered on the platform by accident, became the youngest person to sell out Madison Square Garden and is now worth an estimated $265 million, and the infamous Logan Paul who posted a dead body from Tokyo's "suicide forest", who apparently made about $12.5 million in 2017.

Yeah, that guy made 12.5 million dollars.

Needless to say, YouTube has officially cemented its way into not just to get a lot of subscribers, but also a way to make serious income. And there's a reason why. Who wouldn't want to make 12.5 million dollars a year? So, people flocked to the site, and to this day, people are still trying to get YouTube famous. There are only a few problems with that.

One, the competition is insane. An average of 400 hours of video is uploaded to YouTube every minute. That means that if your video happens to be 5 minutes long, you're competing against 399 hours and 55 minutes' worth of content. That's over one million seconds worth of content. So, this means that you're competing with all of that content, so yours has to be pretty spectacular to stand out.

Two, it's hard work. Yes, the idea of sitting at home and writing and making videos all day may sound like a good time, especially if you're writing about something you love. But, it can be hard work. You had to write the script, usually 2 or 3 times to make sure that it's the best it can be, you have to do any recordings, and then you have to post it. This may not sound like a lot of work, but it can be tough, especially if you're doing it alone.

Third, it can be lonely. One thing that YouTubers are constantly struggling with are feelings of loneliness and worthlessness. Depression is a common problem among them. As a YouTuber, you're often spending long hours alone in front of a computer, and many find themselves obsessing over their amounts of subscribers and putting out content on time. I'm just going to say it: this is the same with a lot of freelance work; the trick is to make sure that you're not letting your entire worth reflect on views and subscribers. Especially make sure that it doesn't take over your entire life. We'll talk more about that later.

Now, this may sound as if I'm trying to talk you out of becoming a YouTuber. Actually, quite the opposite. I'm trying to be honest with you about what you're getting into, and how this will affect your life. You'll be spending long hours in front of a computer, spending a lot of time alone, and not only that, but it can take some time.

There are YouTubers out there who are starting out right now who will be making their living from YouTube in less than 2 years. You could absolutely be one of them. There are stats that work in your favor, after all: Every year, the number of YouTube channels who are making 6 figures worth of income doubles. YouTube accounts for two-thirds of online videos among millennials. Searches of "How To" videos are especially popular; every year, the number of searches increases by 70%.

Those crazy numbers should be what convinces you to take the next step into YouTubing, whether you choose to do it as a full time career or just a part time thing to do for fun. In this book, we're going to tell you how to build a profitable YouTube channel, no matter what your topic. Just know, it may be a bit of an uphill battle.

Now, let's get started.

Make Money on YouTube

Of course, the first thing you need to know about making money off of YouTube, is, well, how exactly do you make money off of YouTube.

We're going to start off this book by talking about how to build your profile, the things you'll need, what your day to day will look like, things like that. Knowing how to manage all of these things will really help you create an effective, money making YouTube channel. After all, even if you're just getting into YouTube because you want to spend your day talking about what you love, or making content that you'd want to see, making money would still be nice.

So, here we are going to list all the ways you can make money. We'll be getting into several of them in more depth in later chapters, so here is just a very brief overview.

1) Use monetization. Monetization from ads has gotten more difficult in the past few years. YouTube, in an effort to take out bad apples in their community, has removed the ability to monetize for a lot of YouTubers. Advertisers now have the ability to choose what kind of content their ads appear on.

2) Use it to bring traffic to your own website or blog. There are plenty of YouTube channels out there, especially recipe or beauty ones, who also have blogs on top of their channel. YouTube is a great place to show off some of your content while keeping the rest on your blog.

3) Sell products. One way that a lot of businesses out there have done is to create products and sell them online. Many YouTubers has taken this step to make extra income, and

some have just started to YouTube just to promote their brand.

4) Do affiliate marketing. If making your own products isn't really your deal, affiliate marketing is the way to go. We'll have an entire chapter dedicated to this later on, but for these who don't know here's a textbook definition: affiliate marketing is the act of you talking about a product from a company on your channel and for every person who goes to buy that product, you get a cut from that company.

5) Crowdfund. This is becoming more and more popular these days, especially with the introduction of websites such as Kickstarter, Patreon, and Indiegogo. It can be a great source of money, but it only works if you have truly good content and a large enough following. You really need to sell your ideas if you want to do this and be able to sell an idea. But, it is a great way to revenue projects for the future. More and more YouTubers are turning to this idea as using ad monetization to make money gets more and more difficult.

We'll be getting farther into each of these topics later on this book, but let's just get this out of the way: you don't have to just do one of the things on this list. In fact, many YouTubers choose to partake in more than one. Having your own stream of revenue that is completely in your hands depends on you looking into as many different forms as possible. Now, it's time to really get down to the important stuff.

In the following chapter, we're going to be talking all about making your channel, your google page, all of the equipment you'll need, skills you may need, and a comprehensive guide to all of YouTube's amazing features. Let's go.

CHAPTER 2
Making Your Channel

You're not going to get anywhere on YouTube without knowing how to build your profile, knowing the kind of skills and equipment you're going to need, and understanding exactly what a YouTube account can give you. Without these things, you're going to get nowhere. That's just a fact.

So, the first thing before you get started with making a YouTube channel, you're going to have to make a Google account. There are plenty of amazing features that Google has to offer, including Google Drive, Google Plus, and of course YouTube.

Thankfully, signing up for an account is an easy and quick process, and you can't get anywhere without on, at least on YouTube. Follow the easy steps below:

1. Open the google webpage. You can do it from the main Google page (google.com) but you can also do it from other places such as Gmail, Google Plus, Google Drive, YouTube, or whatever other pages you can think of. Just simply click on the sign up button, which will take you to another page, where you'll start to input your information.

2. Come up with your username. This username is different from your YouTube channel name. This is what you will use to make your new Gmail email address. You can't create a YouTube page without a Gmail account. If you've already chosen your channel name, use that. Be prepared to change it in case it's already been taken (Google will provide you with similar options if this happens).

3. Put in your information. Enter your first and last name, your gender, your birthday, your country of residence, your phone number for verification purposes, and another email address for more verification.

4. Agree to the privacy policy. Check the box that you agree.

5. Click next. The next page will be your Google plus creation page. This is where you add a picture to your account and write in some information about yourself.

6. Get started. Quickly click the "get started" and you're golden! Just be sure to verify your account.

Now that you've got a Google account! Take your time to adjust yourself to all of their features, including the drive (this will be a great place to keep scripts and collaborate with other YouTubers!) and Gmail (if you so choose, your followers can contact you here!).

Now, let's get into the real fun: creating your YouTube channel.

Now, to be clear, you technically already have a YouTube channel. You get one automatically the minute that you get a Google account. But, you're going to need a business channel if you're there to make content. The process is incredibly simple, and there's only a few clicks and typing involved.

Simply go to your YouTube page, and click on the user icon at the top right of the screen. You want to go to settings, which is the gear icon. There you'll find "create a new channel". Simply click on it, and then find "use a business or other name". Simply add your channel name.

The most important thing to remember about creating your brand name is that it must be short and sweet, or at least catchy. Something that will be remembered easily. Remember, this is not your username, so you don't have to input numbers unless you feel you absolutely have to. Just be sure that it's unique (checking this only requires a quick google search), and go right ahead.

Next, it's time to start filling out your profile.

The first option you see after your channel's creation will be your channel description aka your "About Me". This is where you'll describe your channel, including what you're going to be posting and what your brand is all about. You should also be posting your social media links, any website you may have, and your email where people can get a hold of you. This will be appearing in more than one place on your channel, so make sure to make sure it's good, and regularly update it as time goes on and things change.

Next, put your channel art up.

Go to any professional YouTube channel in the world, and you're greeted with a large banner at the top of their profile displaying the channel's name, plus a design that represents who the brand is. This is known as your banner art, and you can make it as extravagant or as minimal as you wish. The most important thing you can do here is showcase who you are as a brand.

To be sure that you're getting the right sized image, YouTube's recommendation is 2560 x 1440 pixels, the maximum size file being 4 MB. They also offer a template that you can use as your base on their help page. Simply google "YouTube channel banner template" and you'll get many different results. You don't have to be a Grade A designer to have a good one. There are plenty of amazing photo apps that you can use out there. PicMonkey, which is online and can be used from a computer, is a great one. You could also consider hiring a graphic designer, but I would only consider that if you have the cash to spend.

Now, you have your YouTube channel. But, before we get to posting, let's go over some of the other things you'll probably need. For one, you'll need to know your niche. We're going to get into that next chapter, as we're just focusing on the practical stuff here. So, let's get into what you need to make sure your videos are the best they can be.

What you need to make truly great videos on YouTube is greatly over exaggerated. A lot of YouTubers like to show off their fancy cameras and their amazing studios and some of them even have a camera crew. This is not needed, or used, by the majority of YouTubers. In fact, many of them just choose to use their smartphones. If you have a great personality, and your content is truly one of a kind and well put together, you can get away with that. Lots of amazing equipment doesn't necessarily equal good quality content. In fact, many beginner YouTubers (and filmmakers, for that matter) make this mistake and buy expensive equipment, and their videos/films are still not great because they never learned how to use the basic stuff first.

Not only that, but a lot of YouTubers out there will tell you to just focus on the simple stuff when you're just starting out. Why invest a ton of money into something that might not be making you a ton of money for the foreseeable future?

But, then again, we've already talked about how incredibly competitive YouTube is. It's a platform that is built on competitiveness. Whoever gets the most views gets the most money; that's how it works. What does this mean? That you most likely can't get away with just using your smartphone to make videos. Good quality is good quality, and to make truly good videos, you will need to invest at least a little bit of money.

How much you invest is based on two things: the type of content you plan on bringing into this world, and how much money you're willing to put into it. I don't know your financial situation, but I'm going to say this: pick a budget, stick to it, and be practical. Don't buy anything unless you're absolutely sure you're going to need it. That's all, carry on, and here's the list:

- Camera
- Tripod
- Microphone/sound equipment (optional)
- Lighting
- Video Editing Software (optional)

Again, what you buy off this list is entirely up to your choosing. If you want to buy a $4,000 camera, spend $800 on a tripod, and invest in a complete sound and lighting studio, that's up to you. I'm going to advise against it if you still don't know how much money you're going to be able to make, but again, it's up to you.

Now, let's get a little more into each of these things:

Camera

This is 100% the most important piece of equipment you will buy for your channel. Even if you don't plan on having a channel where you appear on camera, I would strongly advise that you at least have access to something that can record high quality video (at least 1080p).

Now, don't just straight away buy an expensive DSLR or mirrorless. These are great for investments later down the road where you're ready for an upgrade. For now, you should probably stick to a quality camcorder or webcam, depending on what your needs are.

Microphone/Sound Equipment

You need good sound. That's just a fact. While you could get away with bad camerawork, you won't be able to get away with bad sound. If you're audio is terrible, it will ruin the whole thing. That's just a fact. While many cameras come with an internal microphone, and it will probably serve you well, it gets more tricky if your video is heavily relying on your dialogue. Not only that, but mics that are built into cameras or laptops usually are not able to record or eliminate ambient sounds effectively. Make sure to do some research into good mics, and ask the person at your local tech store for more information. For YouTubers, USB microphones are the most popular, easy to use and are generally affordable. Of course, there are other options on the market, such as shotguns, and lavaliers, but you may want to upgrade to these later on as they can be more expensive.

Tripod

Tripods are a game changer if you want to create quality content. Unsteady footage can turn your viewers off of watching your content. Another option is something called a Gimbal Stabilizer, which is a lot easier to carry around than a tripod. This, of course, will depend on what kind of content you'll be making, but tripods are generally more affordable. This would be one area where I really press that you invest your money, considering that you need them to be durable and sturdy. This ensures the safety of whatever equipment you're using. A gimbal, on the other hand, is perfect for vlogging. They're stabilizers built specifically with weights or motors, and carefully balance your camera. This makes your videos look more smooth, and even if you make sudden movements, it will still remain smooth. Gimbals only do what they're supposed to do if you have a lightweight camera, like a GoPros. While you can find more heavy duty ones, they're generally a lot more expensive.

Lighting

I would say lighting is only necessary if you find yourself without a good spot to shoot that has no good daylight shining through, or the only times that are available to you are when it's dark out. Or, if you can afford it. Lighting, like sound, is pretty powerful. It can create moods, and even out your whole videos. There are plenty of different kinds of lighting out there, and I would recommend extensive research before you make a choice. You might not even need it at all. I certainly wouldn't tell a beginner YouTuber that they absolutely must need it.

Video Editing Software

I know what you're thinking: why did you label this as optional? Of course, you need good editing software to make good videos. I'm not saying you don't. What I'm debating is whether or not you need to purchase it.

There is no point in buying a program like Adobe Premiere Pro or Apple's Final Cut Pro unless you actually know how to use it, or need to use it. There are plenty of programs that will do all that editing for you that don't cost ridiculous amounts of money and that can do everything that you need. This is especially important to realize if your videos won't require a lot of really complicated editing, like color correcting and being able to process and edit huge, feature movie length files.

Not only that, but video editing programs definitely have a learning curb to them. I'm not saying that you shouldn't learn how to use them, you probably should, but just get used to posting content on your channel first. Once you have gotten into the groove of editing, then you can try something else. Adobe Premiere Pro is a great place to start, and it costs about $20 (USD) a month.

And that's pretty much it for things you'll need to get started on your YouTube channel. Now, just having these items doesn't automatically mean you know how to use them. That's the next step; the skills you need.

Running a YouTube channel will take a bit of a learning curb. Things like being able to organize your time and understand all of YouTube's features will you be able to run a successful YouTube channel. Of course, you can probably run a YouTube channel without a few of the skills mentioned below, but if you want to make money, you'll make more this way.

1) You need to understand the platform. While we're going to go into every single inch of the platform and how it works in this book, it's important to understand that you need to understand it. While this is hardly a complicated platform, there's still a lot to learn.

2) Keyword research. Any YouTuber that puts out quality content on a weekly basis understands that they need to do research, and do it well. You're going to have to spend a lot of time on conversation sites such as reddit, and pay attention to what's going on online in your niche. Not only that, but understanding keyword research will help your videos get the maximum amount of views thanks to search results.

3) Video editing. This is a no brainer. While some YouTubers choose to hire a production team including a camera crew and editing people, your budget may not allow for that at this moment. For editing programs, don't go any more complicated than you feel you need to go. For beginners,

using something like iMovie or VideoPad, both of which are perfect for people who don't have much experience editing videos. Of course, if you do choose to go for the bigger software, there are plenty of tutorials online which will be able to help you out.

4) How to use a camera (properly). If you just plan on using a basic camcorder or a phone this shouldn't be a huge deal but if you're going all out for a DSLR, understanding things like shutter speed, ISO, and white balance will help you out in making sure your videos look amazing.

5) Use of other social media accounts. We're going to talk more about this in this book on how to promote your videos onto other social media accounts, but it is of vital importance. Even if you're just available on one or two other websites, you'll be able to reach a wider audience. What social media presence you choose to use it up to you, but it will depend on your niche. For example, beauty and fashion will find more success on Instagram and Snapchat, while gamers will do better on Twitter and Twitch.

6) Willingness to work hard with endless patience. While there are YouTube channels that grew big within only six months of being on the platform, other big channels took 10 years to get big. It really depends on two things: luck, and your content. There's a lot of amazing content on YouTube. You can't deny that. So, going big often depends on your luck rather than your skills. That doesn't mean that you can't make money off the platform before you gain 1 million followers. It just means that you may have to get creative and be willing to put in some very hard work.

Now, that we've gotten these necessary skills out of the way, let's talk about all of YouTube's great features that they have.

YouTube's Features

Of course, this isn't a complete list of all of the features that YouTube has. I didn't bother with the ones that are obvious, like uploading videos and things. This is more these features that people don't bother taking the time to explore, but are important to you as a content creator, as they'll drastically impact the number of views that you get.

You must keep in mind that for a lot of features that YouTube has, such as monetization, live streaming, and making longer videos, you do have to get verified to do this. The verifying process usually isn't that hard: you can use your cell phone number, or you may have to take YouTube's creator's course to get it. This is so YouTube knows that you're serious about the content you post, and you're not going to fill their airways with spam.

So, now that we've gotten that out of the way, let's get into it:

1) Cards and End Screens. The majority of popular YouTube channels utilize this feature and even the not so popular ones. They work similar to call to action buttons, and they can direct people to subscribe, look at merchandise, or a fundraising campaign. End screens are easily customizable; all you have to do is go to video manager, select "edit", before clicking on "end screen and annotations" from the drop-down menu. Easy. This is where you can play with different backgrounds and templates. To choose where you plan on sending your viewers, you just have to click "add element". This will take you to a list of videos. As for cards, which are found by simply clicking the "I" in the in right hand upper corner of your screen, the card expands and will give you a link to another video or a product. To add a card, simply head to your Video Manager, click edit, and choose cards from the menu. From there, you decided where in the

video you want the card to appear, and what you want it to appear.

2) Creator Studio. There aren't too many creators that actually use the creator studio, but it's full of useful things. You'll find advanced video editing techniques that can usually only be found in programs like Final Cut Pro and Adobe Premiere Pro, such as color correction, time lapse, and slow motion. It also has a huge array of sounds available, free to use for any YouTuber. You won't find any big artists, but you'll definitely find music that matches the tone you're looking for.

3) Live streaming. One of these things that more YouTubers need to be aware of, live streaming is a great way to get more subscribers and create a connection with the ones that you already have. With the introduction of other live streaming platforms like Periscope, Facebook Live, and Instagram Live, it's only going to become more popular. Live streaming on YouTube is slightly more difficult than other websites. You have to download software and set it up first. To get the software, log into YouTube, click the "live-streaming" button on the right hand side of the screen. Click "get started". YouTube will make sure your channel is verified, and you'll have two options, "Stream now" and "Live Events". Which one you pick is up to you, but "Stream now" is the more popular option. You may also stream from mobile devices, but you need 10,000 subscribers to do so.

4) YouTube advanced settings. In YouTube advanced, you can do many things to help get more views to your channel. One of these is you can add your channel keywords. Basically, any word that has anything to do with your channel goes there. You can also go to channel recommendations and click on "allow my channel to appear in other channel's recommendations". This means that YouTube will actually

allow your videos to appear in recommendation lists. You can also see your Google Analytic. You have to connect your YouTube ID to your Google Analytics page, but this lets you see all sorts of information, like what time people are most active on your channel and how long they usually spend on it. This can be useful information when you're choosing what content to put up.

5) Custom URL. If you want to have an easy-to-remember internet link to get your channel, having a custom URL is a great way to go. You can use pretty much anything you want for this, but there are some catches. One, you need 100 subscribers, be at least 30 days old, have channel art, and a profile picture. You also need to be sure that that's what you want for your custom URL. You can't change it afterward. Simply go to YouTube settings and click on advanced in your name section. If you're eligible to get a custom URL, it will tell you under channel settings. Simply agree to their terms of service and click "change URL" to make it official.

Basically, these are all the basic technical stuff you need to know...for now. Of course, you're probably not wanting to get into YouTube to be technical. You're getting into YouTube to chat about all the things that you love. Well, that's what the next chapter is going to be all about: how to find your niche, your audience, and all the different kinds of videos you can make.

CHAPTER 3
Finding Your Voice

When you first start out on YouTube, it can be easy to just post whatever you want, but this really doesn't work with audiences. When audiences follow you on YouTube, they want to know exactly what kind of content to expect from you. You may be a person with a lot of different passions and a lot of different things that you want to talk about, but that doesn't work for audiences.

This means that you have to find your niche, and you have to stick to it. I would say before you've even posted your first video, you should have your first 10 planned out and prepared. I'm serious. Having all of your videos planned out, and prepared will give you a lot of breathing room of getting used to YouTube, and not only that but give you some time to prepare for the next ten. Having a plan will really help you adjust more easily and get you into the flow of posting.

But first, let's talk about your niche. Here are just a few tips on how to find a topic that you want to talk about day to day.

5 Tips On Finding Your Niche

1) Make a list of all the topics that you love. This is a topic that you're going to be spending a lot of time discussing, thinking about, and making videos about it. People will be subscribing to your channel based on the topic that you eventually land on to make your channel about.

2) Choose a niche with a lot of subtopics. This is a mistake that a lot of beginner YouTubers make, where their niche is so strict and solid that they cannot get more than maybe 50 videos out of it. Your niche topic should be broad enough

that there are plenty of subtopics to address. For example, let's say that your chosen niche is "lifestyle". Well, this can mean things like health, fitness, beauty, remodeling, parenting, finance, and a variety of other topics.

3) Make sure it's either something you're well versed in or you want to become well versed in. Now, to be clear, there are plenty of YouTubers out there who are far from experts on their chosen topic. In fact, a lot of their charm is in the fact that they're learning as they go along. You're a beginner, just like your audience. Now, the downside of choosing a topic that you don't know much about is the fact that the amount of research goes up considerably, so if you're not willing to spend all that time researching that topic, don't do this. You need to be able to put content out there that is correct, as this will be the key to making sure that your channel gets the attention that it needs to grow.

4) Look into what other people are doing (and do it better). One thing that makes people turn away from starting a channel is the fact that there is already so much content out there. But, this can also be a good thing. If you can find a side that hasn't been addressed yet, jump on that. Not only that, but if you want to make a film review channel, and there are people who love to watch film reviews, they're not likely to just go to one source for them. They want a bunch of different sources. If you can do something differently from anyone else, that content will be valuable.

5) Find an idea that nobody else is doing. If out of one of your ideas there's an idea that nobody else is doing, jump on that. If there is no competition, you have struck gold. This doesn't mean that you have to have a completely new idea. You just have to have an idea that is different from all the rest, one with a twist. You just have to find a gap that hasn't been covered yet.

6) Try to solve problems. The search for "how to" videos goes up higher and higher every year. And besides that, every single popular web page or YouTube video in the history of the internet goes back to some kind of need. Vlogs, it's a feeling of needing to be a part of their life. For review channels, it's the feeling of your choices needing to be valid. YouTube isn't about you. It's about fulfilling the needs of somebody out there. Keep that in mind, and finding your niche and starting your channel will be off to a great start.

What Kind Of Videos Do I Want To Make

Now, I know what you're thinking. Isn't the niche the same thing as the type of videos I want to make?

Well, yes and no. Yes, because a niche can definitely decide what kind of videos you'll be posting, but sometimes, there is a wide variety of things you'll be posting. Let's say you want to talk about movies. Are you going to be analyzing them? Reviewing them? Doing top 10 lists? What?

So, to help you get some ideas, here are the top 20 videos that get the most views on the platform. Don't feel as if you have to make these types of videos to get a lot of views, but it definitely doesn't hurt to have these on hand for yourself.

1) Product reviews. I was shocked that it wasn't cat videos. Straightforward product videos are basically just a person in front of a video talking about what they think of a certain product. The more brutally honest, the better. Anything from technology (which is the most popular) to movies to make up to restaurants can be done. Why are they so popular? Well, more and more people are turning to the internet to know other people's reviews on products. They're much more likely to trust an online influencer with

thousands of subscribers who haven't been paid off by the company, rather than an ad that is made to make the product look like the best product ever. This makes a lot of sense.

2) How Tos/Tutorials: the second most popular search engine in the world is YouTube, and one of the most popular searched things on the web is "how tos". If there is something that you can do well, you may have a future in YouTube tutorials.

3) Vlogs: blogs, but in video form. Quick, fun, and casual, they can cover a variety of topics of day to day life. They're usually more on the light side but can delve into more serious topics, and many do.

4) Gaming: this kind of YouTubing is often looked down upon, thanks to the eternal question "why would you want to watch someone playing when you could just do it yourself?" Well, there isn't really an answer to this question, but you can't deny how popular the concept is on the website. YouTube even launched a site just for video game streams, that's how big it is.

5) Comedy/Skit Videos: this is another comedy niche that can be hard to make money off of, but they can be fun to make. You can also raise money for them through Kickstarter. These can really go from anything to improvised silly bits to full on productions.

6) Hauls: these videos have no middle ground, they're either loved or hated by a person. Basically, you go out and buy a bunch of stuff, then show off what they bought in a video. Not only that but once you get enough views, you won't have to buy anymore, as brands send you things for free in hopes you'll talk about them.

7) Memes/Tags/Challenges: these can be varied, and will go from very silly to more serious. Draw-my-life, the boyfriend tag, cinnamon challenge, ice-bucket challenge, and more. You could even start your own and see if it takes off.

8) Favorites/Best Of: in this kind of video, you basically showcase what your favorite things are, based on a certain topic, or what the best of the best is. It can be anything from what your favorite movies are to what are the best makeup brands there are right now. Anything goes.

9) Education: pretty self-explanatory. These are just videos that are made with the intent of someone learning from them on a particular topic. Bonus points if you can make them easy to digest and designed for students.

10) Unboxing: basically, if you enjoy shopping and love unboxing things, this is for you. Any product can be unboxed on camera, and people will want to watch it. You generally have to have an idea of what kind of products you'll be unboxing (toys, technology, makeup, clothes, etc.). People like to watch these because it shows them exactly what to expect when they order something.

11) Q & A be online long enough, and eventually, your followers are going to want to know more about you. This is a great way to interact with your following. Simply ask your followers for questions, usually through Facebook, Twitter, or Instagram, and pick the best ones to answer in a video.

12) Collections: really not much to say here. Just a person showing off their collection of whatever items they collect, whether it's a single type or a group based on a theme. They then explain where the item comes from.

13) Pranks: Pranks aren't nearly as popular on YouTube as they were back in the day, but they're still there. Anything from super intense, controversial stunts to staged jokes done with

other creators to silly, simple practical jokes are on the website.

14) Funny animals: there aren't a lot of people who can see a picture of a cute dog or a cute cat doing something silly and not at least smile. It's just not possible. Cute and funny; nothing bad here.

15) Celebrity Gossip: this can be a big difficult to break into, but if you can, do it. It also takes a lot of research, and you risk the chance of a lawsuit if you get something really wrong. However, just because of these, doesn't mean you shouldn't give it a try if you're willing. People may like to say that they're above celebrity gossip, but the majority of them really aren't.

16) Parodies: these are very popular on YouTube mostly thanks to the fact that people want to laugh. But, it's a lot harder to make money off of them, with many trying to profit but very few of them actually doing so. This is something that you should only do if you're going to actually have fun doing so.

17) Self Improvement: this is pretty much self-explanatory. These videos are meant to help people improve themselves in sometimes simple, sometimes complicated ways. They can address topics like nutrition, self-love, and how to handle depression.

18) Covers: Nobody who is in the YouTube world can forget the fact that YouTube took a 12 year old kid living in a small Canadian town named Justin Bieber to international stardom. It's because of this that many other musicians have taken to the platform to promote their own music, usually by covering popular songs.

19) Couple Vlogs: think of that one couple that you know that is super cute and everyone tells them so, and pick up the phone and tell them they may have what it takes to become

a successful couples vlog channel. They do things like post about their dates, their adventures together, couples tags, and day to day life. The type of videos that make you feel all fuzzy inside.

20) Cooking: cooking channels that show recipes step by step are popular, mostly thanks to the amount of creativity they allow. Creative channels are big on YouTube, especially ones that do things you're not expecting. Tasty, which is owned by Buzzfeed, is especially known for putting out some crazy food ideas. Not only that, but who doesn't want to learn how to cook easy, some healthy, some not-so-healthy, and delicious recipes?

The Importance of Quality of Quantity

Quality over Quantity is a concept that was probably taught to you when you were a child. But, it's hard to adjust to, especially in today's world where putting out as many products as possible is what you're supposed to be doing. It's widely regarded as the quicker you can put out content, the more money you will make.

While this is true, and this is a system that many companies have implemented in an effort to make as much money in the shortest amount of time. This is the best business model: the quicker you can make a product, the more money you will save and the more money you will make. Unfortunately, crafting products that are high quality are expensive and time consuming, and if your goal is to put out content as fast as possible, you may find yourself running yourself dry.

But, when you're putting out content like video content, quality is so important. Bad audio, blurry videos, crappy lighting, bad research, all of these things will degrade the quality of your channel and make people want to go somewhere else for content. This is the last thing that you want. You want a channel that generating revenue, and to do that, you need people to actually watch your channel.

So, try to only upload one video a week, at least at first. That means you can put all of your time, energy, and money into making that video the best of the best. Every video that is sent out you should have the feeling of "I gave it my all". While there are plenty of businesses out there that can get away with not following this philosophy, YouTube is not one of them. Don't ignore it.

CHAPTER 4
Growing

Of course, you won't have any success on YouTube without doing the one most important thing: and that's posting. But don't just go crazy and start posting videos right now.

What a lot of beginner YouTubers don't realize is that there are not only ways to make posting easier for you, but also ways to make sure that it's getting the most views as it can possibly get. There are more effective ways to post, and in this chapter, I'm going to tell you how.

Other things in this chapter are reasons why, that despite numerous people doing it, you probably shouldn't be buying YouTube subscribers, no matter how much of an easy shortcut it is. Not only that, but we're going to talk about how you can grow organically, plus a guide in how to get past that creative block if you ever find yourself struggling. Let's get started, shall we?

Guide to Posting Effectively

Read this simple guide to uploading if you don't care about views or money:

1. Log into your account. If it's from the Google homepage, click on the YouTube icon in the corner.

2. Select the upload button. It's in the top right corner at the beginning, a silhouette of a video camera with a plus sign.

3. You have two options on how to go from here: you can drag and drop the file, or you can select to upload.

4. Enter the description, tags, privacy information, and add a thumbnail if you want to.

5. Share the video.

That's it. Simple, right? YouTube is designed to be simple, after all.

Now, let's go through all these steps one by one, shall we? Especially if you want to make some money.

Now, before we get into the actual posting, let's first start with this easy fact: timing.

When you choose to upload a video, your timing actually matters, believe it or not. This occurs on every social media page: there is always the best time to post so your blog/page/video/post/picture gets the most views, likes, comments, and basically engagement possible.

For YouTube, thankfully there is always a model you can follow, and that's TV. When does TV air the most episodes? Nighttime. When does all their prime content air? Usually weekend times, from Thursday to Sunday. People generally are more likely to check out YouTube during the weekends (or in the evenings) because that is when they're home and scrolling through their feed looking for something to watch.

Thursday and Friday have proven to be the best, with it starting to spike up on Thursday, before peaking on Saturday and dying down on Sunday. This is as people prepare for their week. Of course, this is up to you when you want to post.

The next thing you need to really worry about is step 4. This is where you basically set all the settings of your video. There are privacy settings, the thumbnail, adding your tags, and putting it into a playlist (if you so choose).

YouTube offers four different privacy settings; unlisted, private, public, and schedule. Private is obvious, meaning that only you can see it. Unlisted means that only people with whom you have a link to the video that you can see it.

Public means that anyone can view or search for the video. They can share it as much as they want. Any subscribers you have will see it in their feed. This is the obvious choice for YouTubers. But the schedule is honestly the one that I'm going to discuss here.

Schedule means that you can set a time and date for when you want your video to go public. This means that you could literally have weeks of content in your folder and simply schedule it, meaning that you won't have to worry about anything, just coming up with ideas.

Then, we're going to talk about filling out your description, tags, etc. You can fill out a lot of this information while you're uploading, actually, which will save you a bit of time.

Title: Quick and simple. As you're filling this out, remember this. Keep it simple. The shorter, the better. Just stick to what exactly your video is. When people search for your video; that is what your title should be. At least less than 10 words.

Description: If there is something that you can't squeeze into the title, this is where you can put it. Really consider keywords here, as descriptions will also register on YouTube's and Google's search bar, and don't forget to make it really long and descriptive. The more words you hit, the more likely you are to show up on Google. You should also include any links to important information, such as your other social media pages or business email, here. To make this process easier for you, you can add defaults for whenever you upload in Settings. Under YouTube's advanced settings, you can set a description template, meaning that you won't have to fill it all out every time, making the process a lot more streamlined.

Tags: similar to posting on Instagram or Twitter, using tags is an easy way to help users find your videos easily. Keywords will be especially valuable here, with single words being more effective that full sentences.

Thumbnail: this is a mistake that too many beginner YouTubers make, not using a custom thumbnail. While YouTube will supply you with thumbnails (3 of them, to be exact) once enough of your video has uploaded, they're hardly good ones, and will only be screenshots of your video. This means that they can be very unflattering. A customized thumbnail gives you the option of including whatever you want in your thumbnail, including text, a good image, and more. The only thing is that you have to verify your account before seeing the thumbnail option, which is not a hard thing to do. You can find this in settings.

Add to Playlists: having playlists on your channel is a good way to keep your channel organized, but it also helps with keeping your users engaged, keeping them watching your videos, rather than it auto playing to something else. Say you're a movie reviewer, and you organize your reviews based on the genre. That means someone who is really into that genre can watch each on in a row without having to bother clicking the next video. Many popular channels use this system, separating them based on everything from what their content is to their length to who made it.

Now, these are the basic settings that you can set. Now, a lot of YouTubers don't really take advantage of all of YouTube's advanced settings. I still think you should check them out, even if you don't find anything that you're interested in tinkering with. If there are certain settings that you'd want for all of your videos, you can set them to defaults in advanced settings.

In this section, you can do the following things:

Disable comments: I wouldn't honestly recommend this because I think that comments can be valuable to YouTubers. This is the most direct form of communication with your audience that you have. But there are situations that call for it. If there is a certain video that you don't want to get hate comments on, consider deactivating them.

Categories: YouTube has 18 different categories your video can fall into: Auto & Vehicles, Beauty & Fashion, Comedy, Education, Entertainment, Family Entertainment, Film & Animation, Food, Gaming, How-to & Style, Music, News & Politics, Nonprofits & Activism, People & Blogs, Pets & Animals, Science & Technology, Sports and Travel & Events. You can pick and choose which one you feel best suits your video. Make sure that whatever category you choose is accurate, as it will help people find you.

Content declaration: this is particularly important if you're going to participate in affiliate marketing. If your video has been sponsored by a company and you're getting paid to talk about them, this must be stated for legal purposes. But this isn't just because of legal reasons: there should always be transparency with an audience when they're watching you, as you're depending on them for views, subscribes, and thumbs up. If there is product placement, endorsement or sponsorship involved you must tell them. Telling them upfront will build an element of trust.

And done! Your video is officially live once it's finished processing! Congrats!

Now, if you're planning on sharing it to other social media networks (which I strongly recommend, and something I'll be talking about soon). Share it to your other social media channels. This is simple: you can either take the URL and directly copy and paste it, or you can use the share button. Another window will pop up, showing you your options where you can share your option. It will also give you a condensed think.

How To Grow YouTube

Of course, the next question is this: how can I grow in a way that's organic and sustainable, that will bring me subscribers who are loyal and watch my videos? Growing on YouTube can seem like a long, crazy, tenuous process that takes years and years. It doesn't necessarily have to be this way; here are some tips on how to speed up this process.

1) Consistency. Consistency, consistency, consistency. One thing that is the most important thing for your audience is that you're consistent with the content that you're bringing to the table, but not just that. You also have to be consistent with your schedule. As in, you always upload on the same day and at the same time. There are YouTubers who post consistently but on random days. This works, but not as well if you're on a schedule. This means that if you always post on Sunday, your subscribers know to look forward to Sunday. See what I mean?

2) Use other social media networks. Look in next chapter for more information on that exact subject!

3) Try keeping videos short and snappy, at least for the first few 10,000 subscribers or so. If you can sum things up in three minutes, do it. You can get into longer videos later when you have a good number of followers involved and interested.

4) Use keywords. Use keywords. Use keywords. That doesn't mean just rattling off whatever words come to mind when you're thinking of in your video description though. Make sure that it actually makes sense.

5) Put a trailer on your channel. Once you have a lot of interesting videos, or even if you just want to take the clips from future videos that you've filmed, put together a trailer for the front page of your channel that's less than 2 minutes long. You can put in at the front of your page and should be treated similarly to a YouTube channel. Introduce yourself and captivate potential subscribers. Ask them to like, comment, and subscribe. You could even ask them a question at the end of your video such as "what do you think"? This really ups your comment count.

6) Use call to actions in your videos. Do you know how every single YouTuber in the history of YouTube asks whoever's watching to subscribe? There's a reason why they do it; it actually works.

7) Engage with your audience. Reply to comments (including negative ones, if you dare). This shows you're paying attention to them. You should be especially paying attention to the ones that are always commenting and liking. Treat your followers well.

8) Collaborate. More on that in Chapter 6!

9) Subtitle and transcribe your videos in your native language, and if you can, any other languages you can. This not only opens up your videos for people who are hearing impaired but also shows up for your international audience.

10) Use annotations and end screens to promote other videos, the channel, or your website. Annotations are useful links that can be made in the creator's studio, basically just leading back to more of your content. Use content that you think your followers will want to watch.

But, what if you don't want to do all this work? Maybe you just want to buy your subscribers and be done with it. That's what we're going to talk about next.

Buying Subscribers

Buying followers, or in this case, subscribers, is a popular tactic online to quickly grow your follower base. Be on any social media network for long enough and you'll likely be contacted by several of them, especially on Instagram. Now, YouTube isn't Instagram, but it's still an important topic to address. The people who will write to you, or the ads that you will see, pertaining to this very subject will claim that "this is the fastest, cheapest way to grow your base!" and that "this is the only way to do this! A shortcut to success!"

So, the question is; should you do it?

I would personally say no. And we'll get into that. But, first, I am going to acknowledge the fact that yes, it can be really tempting to take the easy way out. If you're going to invest into your channel, you may as well just buy followers and views, right? It's easy, fast, and generally affordable. No downsides! Not only that, but many big names in the YouTube are rumored to have done it, with even celebrities such as Beyoncé and Rihanna allegedly being guilty of this.

Not only that, but the whole business of buying/selling YouTube (and other social media networks) subscribers/followers/likes/views is pretty lucrative. There are people pulling in $200,000 a year doing just that, just in case you ever choose to go that route. But buying subscribers has just a few problems, which in my opinion, should lead you to balk:

- YouTube is working on their bot detection capabilities, and they're only going to get better.

- YouTube's algorithm has begun to pay more attention to the behavior of the account rather than how many views the video has.

- It won't bring in money for you.

Basically, what this means is that if you buy fake subscribers, you risk the chance of your channel getting deleted, it may not help you attract new subscribers, and the worst part of all, the followers won't bring in new money for you, because they won't be rewatching your videos, and they won't be buying anything off of you because they're fake. They're not here to learn anything from you.

We all want to grow in the fastest way possible, and we all want to just make it easy on ourselves. After all, hard work, a lot of effort, and your time and money are going into it. You want to get the quickest results possible. But, there are better ways to grow your channel organically than just buying a bunch of fake followers, many of whom we've already run over in this book. You could also consider buying ads if you're really wanting to grow fast.

So, personally, I would balk away from buying followers, especially as YouTube gets smarter about catching accounts that use them. You don't want to build up an incredible, engaged base, and get banned just as things are starting to flow well.

How To Brainstorm Video Ideas

Any YouTuber has been there. You've started out, everything is going great, and after a few weeks or months or even years, the video ideas just stop coming to you. Maybe it's happening over time, or maybe it's just one day, you wake up, and realize you just can't think of anything. Regardless, it's annoying, and now you're stuck.

Creative block happens with any artist, and that's really what a YouTuber is in some way, an artist. You're creating content to be enjoyed by the masses, and you want to create good content. You're often writing, directing, and editing your own videos. So, you have to treat this like an artist would consider a block. Here are some tips on how to come with new video ideas, no matter what your niche is:

1) Use the search result method. This is a simple method that merely involves Google's habit of completing our sentences without asking. When you start to type something into the search bar, Google tries to finish your thought. Simply type in some keywords having to do with your niche, and you'll get some ideas. Not only that, but you'll know what people are looking for. Google's automated suggestions are based on what is looked up for a lot. So, people will already have been looking for your ideas.

2) Check out trends. No matter what your niche is, there will always be trends in whatever it is. Be sure to keep your ear to the ground as to what is happening in your community, and even try to keep up with what's happening in the larger community. This has two benefits. One, you'll be constantly be exposed to content in your niche that might provide you with ideas, and two, by addressing the topics that are on trend in your videos means that you're showing your followers that you're paying attention. Win, win.

3) Search your comments. Once you have been on YouTube or any social media outlook for an amount of time, you're going to start getting comments. And, if your content is good, people will want to see more from you and will offer suggestions in the comments. Some of these ideas are actually really good, so be sure to make this a habit of combing through your comments. If you're not getting

many comments, actually ask your followers for them. They probably have some really good ideas.

4) Ask the people around you. This is very similar to the above one, but if you have close friends or family who watch your videos, then consider asking them. This one is good for newer YouTubers who may not have that many comments.

5) Seek media different from yours. This means that if you review cars, you should check out beauty channels. Yes, I'm serious. Engaging and picking up media that is vastly different from yours will get different parts of your brain going, and will widen your worldview. One of the easiest ways to do this to go to a bookstore, a magazine stand, or even your local library, and seek out materials that are vastly different from yours. There may not be very many ideas for you at first glance, but you just might stumble across something really interesting.

6) Check out the other side. If you're a channel that posts a lot of videos about your opinions (reviews, political content) consider checking out other YouTubers and especially focus on the ones that you don't necessarily agree with. They may cover a topic that you want to cover, or you may want to argue against one of their videos.

7) Ask yourself: what do I want to say? This is the best way to make sure that you're sticking to your original ideas. What do you want to say about your channel? What message do you want to put forward? If you find that this by itself isn't working, try expanding what you want to say.

How to Record Compelling Videos

Finally, how do you create content that will keep your followers coming back for more? How do you keep them watching? How do you do this in a way that will not just keep them watching, but make them want to come back for more and watch more of it? Well, here are some tips.

1) Tell a story. If you're selling something, it's important to focus on the story, not the actual product. If you look at any real ad from the world of advertising, they focus on the emotional pull over the fact that they're selling. Remember the viewer, and pull at their emotional strings. The best way to do this is with a good story.

2) Be relevant. Make sure that every video falls in line with what you are as a channel and your channel. No matter how great the video is put together, it won't be good for your subscriber count if you're not on base. Make sure it's relevant not only to who you are, but who they are as well.

3) Give away information. Social currency is basically just information, something that people can share or use or something that makes them look or feel good.

4) Hook them in 3 seconds. Make it interesting in the first 3 seconds of your videos. This is when new viewers will decide whether or not they're going to watch it. Be description, use catchy titles and music, and have a great opening.

5) Be wary of the times. Right message, right person, right time. Pay attention to what's happening in the world, and embrace what people want and what they're looking for. Your subscribers will be paying attention to current events as well, so they may want to hear from you about certain topics.

And, that's it for posting and creating videos. From here on out, we're mostly going to be talking about how to actually make money on the platform, but first; we're going to talk about two things.

Next, social media and how to utilize it to really grow your channel, and then collaborations, and how to make the most of them.

CHAPTER 5
Leveraging Other Social Media

If there is one way to think of the internet, it's similar to high school. And what does high school have? They have cliques. There are the cheerleaders, the jocks, the nerds, the art kids, the drama kids, and so on. That's just how high school works. They may be some crossover, but for the most part, people usually stick in their lane. They want to be surrounded by people that they know, and who they know to agree with them. We like to say that we have left high school behind, but just look at social media demographics and you know that it's not true.

When you've discovered what your niche is and who you're demographic is, aka who you're making the videos for, and once you've actually started uploading videos, you're going to need to find a way to reach more people in that demographic. This is why selecting the social media network that works for you is so important; different kinds of people are attracted to different kinds of places online.

YouTube is pretty universal. People from every walk of life, whether it's their gender to their sexuality to their religion to their families can have a place on YouTube. It's because of what makes YouTube different from other social media networks on the site; it's a search engine. YouTube is often listed among social media networks, but it's really not. Social media networks, like Facebook, Twitter, and Instagram were designed for the sole reason of maintaining social connections with other people. YouTube was designed for people to create and upload content.

And this is what works for the platform. The demographics of YouTube spans across the entire board. 96% of 18 to 24-year-olds use the platform, but it's not just them. That number is rising among the older generation too. Here is a list of all of the percentage of people, divided by age group, who use YouTube regularly:

25 to 34-year-olds: 95%
35 to 44year-olds: 90%
45 to 54-year-olds: 85%
55 to 64-year-olds: 79%
65 to 75-year-olds: 66%
75+-year-olds: 51%

As you can see, that's a huge group of people who are on the platform. So, finding a demographic on YouTube shouldn't be a huge issue. But, that's not what this chapter is about. This chapter is about where else can you go online to find people with whom your content is aimed at. This is why using other social media channels will help elevate your brand. But this chapter isn't just about finding a social media network that works for you; we're also going to talk about how you can use them (briefly). I would definitely recommend that once this is all over, go out and do research on your chosen social media network. How you approach this could mean the difference between your channel succeeding or failing.

Now, let's get into it. Below, you'll find information on 4 of the biggest social media networks on the planet, plus some quick facts on what to know how each platform works.

Facebook is the one social media platform you really can't ignore. It's the third most visited website in the world and the top most downloaded app for mobile. It's the King of social media, whether you like it or not, and their recent issues with privacy have done nothing to slow it down. It has over 3 billion users worldwide, a third of the population, and 2 and a half billion of these users use it regularly.

This means that if your content is something that appeals to a wide audience, you probably will want to have a Facebook page. This goes without saying. But, Facebook seems to be dying slowly with the younger demographics. Teens and young adults just aren't interested in the platform, and while it still used by their generation, the trend seems to be dying fast. So, if you do have a product that appeals to both the younger and the older generation, you may want to consider having a Facebook account along with something like Instagram or Snapchat, both of which are incredibly popular with the younger generation.

So, here are their age demographics:

18 to 24 years olds: 15%
25 to 34 years olds: 26%
35 to 44 years old: 20%
45 to 54 years olds: 16%
55 to 64 years olds: 13%
65+ years olds: 10%

As for gender:

54% of the platform is women
46% of the platform is men

And here are some other stats:

- 85% of Facebook's daily users are from outside North America.

- About 80% of daily internet users use Facebook.

- 82% of college graduates use Facebook.

- The country with the most amount of Facebook users is not the USA, which has 210 million users. It's India, with 270 million.

- 75% of urban residents are on Facebook, with 67% of suburban residents and 58% of rural residents.

Here are some tips on how to use it:

- Post 1 - 3 times per day. Any more time and you're going to lose your likes.

- Engage and reply back to comments.

- Post behind the scene videos from your shoots; videos and photos get more engagement.

- Ask your followers a lot of questions and engage them with your posts.

Facebook is one of these platforms you really can't ignore, but you can get away with it if you don't want to. While it's definitely a platform that's worth looking into, some people just don't like it, and that's OK.

Instagram is easily one of the hottest websites online, with it just hitting it's 1 billion user mark in 2019. Instagram is the place to go if your content is very visual, or if you're selling products. Instagram is built all around the pictures, so if your content is very engaging and pretty to look at, this is the place to go. After all, you're making videos, your content should already be engaging.

Instagram is also very useful for anyone who wants to sell things. Instagram is all about selling, with influencers making thousands of dollars off a single pretty picture. This is because if people follow others for two reasons: they're personal friends of them, or they want that lifestyle. Instagram is all about showing off what you have, and people tend to like things that they can't have. So, if you can show off your products in an appealing way that really shows off the lifestyle, then Instagram is perfect for you. It's also a great place for vlogs and lifestyle brands.

Let's break down some of the age demographics:

18 to 24 years olds: 39%
25 to 34 years olds: 32%
35 to 44 years old: 15%
45 to 54 years olds: 8%
55 to 64 years olds: 3%
65+ years olds: 2%

As for gender:

50% of the platform is women.
50% of the platform is men.

Instagram is pretty even when it comes to their gender, but you cannot deny that among millennials, it is still hugely popular. Over half of the platform is people under the age of 35, and all of the features only make these numbers keep skyrocketing. Instagram is owned by the company Facebook, so the two platforms work well together for anyone who is looking for fluidity.

Not only that but here are some other stats:

- Out of 1 billion monthly active users, over half of them use the platform daily.

- The average Instagram post gets 4 times more engagement than the average Facebook post, but they spend about the same amount of time, 53 minutes per day.

- 1 in 3 Instagram users have directly used the platform to buy products. 83% of them say they discover new services and products on Instagram.

- 50% of Instagrammers follow online businesses and brands.

To use Instagram, follow these tips:

- Post at least 1 to 3 times per day. Anymore and you'll annoy your followers into not following you unless you're a big time celebrity.

- Use stories. Stories, which was ripped right off of Snapchat, is a great way to get more personal with your followers on top of all of the put together pictures on your feed. Using stories about 3 to 8 times per day is golden, and there are plenty of features that make them fun.

- Use hashtags. Hashtags are one of the easiest ways that people can find you on Instagram. Use them. If you don't want to put them in your main photo, you can instead comment on your picture yourself with all 30 of them. There's no difference in the amount of attention.

- Share your Instagram photos to Twitter, Facebook, and Tumblr (if you have them).

- Edit your photos, but don't use the one inside Instagram. The photos edited there tend to look a bit cheap. Instead, invest in a photo editing app like VSCO or Snapseed. Both of these apps are available on iOS and Google Play Store and are popular with Instagram users.

These tips are easy to follow and should gain you a lot of followers. The most important thing to remember that on Instagram is that engagement is really key. As long as you encourage engagement, you should be golden.

Twitter is all about the "now". Basically, if something is happening right at this very moment, Twitter is the place to go. This is why it's a huge place for things like current events and news. It's also the place where social media marketing got its roots, believe it or not. On Twitter, someone can contact their favorite businesses, content creator, or brand directly, without any barriers. This is why it's huge for businesses, and is the place where the majority of people go when they have something to say directly to a company.

In terms of what kind of people hang out on Twitter and use the platform a lot, this section is all about these things that you should know.

By age, the stats go as follows:

18 to 20 years olds: 4%
21 to 24 years olds: 7%
25 to 34 years olds: 43%
35 to 44 years old: 28%
45 to 54 years olds: 12%
55 to 64 years olds: 3%
65+ years olds: 1%

Teens aged below 18 cannot be counted on the platform. Keep that in mind.

In terms of gender:

70% of the platform is female
30% of the platform is male

Here are some other stats that might solidify your choice:

- Twitter has a huge international base, with 80% of its users based outside of the USA. The three countries with the higher user count (other than the USA) are Brazil, Japan, and Mexico.

- Almost half, about 46% of their users are on the platform daily.

- A third of Americans aged 18 to 29 years old, about 36% of them, use Twitter.

Here's how to use twitter to help grow your YouTube channel:

- Tweet anywhere from 3 to 6 times a day. Just continually updating your followers about your day, from how a video shoot is going, to how writing a script, to asking them questions, anything goes.

- Engage with your followers. Reply to them. Twitter is the perfect place where users can reach you and talk to you directly, so use it that way.

- Use all their features. You can run polls on Twitter, and make lists. Use them both.

- Engage with other creators. Twitter isn't just a great place for your fans to be reaching you, it's also a great place for you to reach your favorite YouTubers. Do it! You may get some collaborations out of it.

Twitter is the perfect customer service website, and if you want to engage directly with your followers, plus if your niche is in that demographic, go for it. It's perfect for you.

Snapchat is the place to be if you're trying to appeal to teens. That's basically it. I'm not going to talk too much about what the age demographics are too much in this, but if you're trying to appeal to teens (or anyone under 25) Snapchat is the place to be. Over 70% of people under 30 use the platform for some reason or another, and it's not very common with anyone over that age.

Snapchat is at its core a messaging service. Known for its "snaps", picture messages that disappear after usually about 10 to 15 seconds, it now has about 180 million users, and the majority of them are under 30 (easily about 70%). It's more popular with women, but the gender specifics are very even, with about 60% of women using the platform, while 40% of men. Here are some other stats:

- 69% of 13 to 17 year olds use Snapchat, while 68% of 18 to 29 year olds.

- The average Snapchat user visits about 25 times a day, spending about 40 minutes on the platform.

- It's more popular with higher income adults, with 30% of adults with an income of $75,000 per year using it. In contrast, only 23% of adults with an income of less than $30,000 per year use it.

To use Snapchat, follow these tips:

- Post to your story often.

- Use all of their features (gifs, stickers, etc.).

- Hold a Q & A session.

- Show a lot of behind-the-scenes shots.

- Do announcements and special offers.

- Don't be too perfect and put together. This is a big one. Snapchat stories are a lot more personal than other platforms like Instagram or Facebook, so you need to be more personal. It's what your followers expect. This means blurry videos, no makeup pictures, stuff like that. Just be personal.

I know what you're thinking, this isn't nearly the amount of advice you got for the other social media platforms, but that's really the point. Snapchat is very simple in how it works, and very straightforward. It's all about taking your followers through your day, so just bring them through your day. Your imperfect, messy day.

Now, using at least one or two of these social media will really help bring attention to your channel in a good way. There is a whole group of people on these platforms that have never heard of your channel that you can appeal too. Plus, you'll make money faster. Win, win.

CHAPTER 6
Guide To Collaboration

Collaboration. What is collaboration?

Collaboration is the act of working together with another YouTuber, ideally one who is also in your niche. It's a technique used by a ton of YouTubers online, and you'll often see them doing it on their channels. It's beneficial to everyone, a tit for tat idea so to speak. It's easily one of the best ways to build your YouTube channel and subscriber list.

Collaborating is not just a way to build subscribers. It's also an easy way to stay connected to other YouTubers on the platform. By doing collaborations with other YouTubers that your followers subscribe to and enjoy, you're showing that you're paying attention. Even if you just do a collaboration with a YouTuber that nobody has ever heard of (it's the internet, it's a big place), you still show that you're a part of your community. It shows you live outside of your own little bubble of the internet.

The basic fact is, collaboration is a good thing to get into the habit of doing on your channel. In this chapter, we're going to discuss not only all the reasons you should be doing YouTuber collaboration, but also how to get one done in a way that will be smooth for you, and how to find people to collaborate with.

Why Collaboration Works Well

Why should you collaborate with other YouTubers? A lot of people get into YouTubing because they want to be alone, because they don't want to be talking and communicating with other people. To be completely fair, you probably could build your YouTube channel without collaboration and only ever communicating with your followers through a camera and a laptop, but I would advise against it. Collaboration is hugely beneficial for everyone involved. Let's just count a few of the ways.

- You reach their subscriber base. This is an obvious one, and one of the biggest reasons why YouTubers started up collaborations in the first place. When you appear on someone else's channel, or when they appear on yours, you are immediately exposed to an entirely new group of followers. If you're working with someone in your niche and who has the same audience as you, these people are very likely to be potential subscribers for you. This is easily the most basic reason why you should be collaboration; you can build up your base hugely this way.

- It shakes things up. It's something different for your current base to watch. It's something that's fresh and offbeat. Collaboration usually opens the doors for you to do something different. It's not just your head anymore. It offers you a lot of different ways to approach things.

- It helps creativity. This is similar to the last reason, but it's still important. Collaboration is all about that; collaboration. This means that you're working together with someone, and they may not think the same way you do. They may challenge you to see something differently. This can be a great thing for your channel. You may come up with some video ideas that you never would've thought of alone, and this can inspire you in general for your channel.

- It helps you build relationships. It's really important to be an active part of your community on the internet, especially if you're trying to get people to pay attention to you. Hanging out on the forums, responding to comments and questions, these things are great, but actually working with other people shows that you're paying attention to your community. Whether they're up and comers or people who have posted more than 5,000 videos, working with other people gives this impression that you're open to building these relationships. They can just be working relationships if you wish, but the internet is great at bringing people together if nothing else. You'll get along really well with a lot of these people, and you might find yourself with good friends, who you will want to work with again and again.

- It shows you care. Not just about views and subscribers, but about your base. Scroll through your comments enough times, and you'll find that there probably are a few requests for a collaboration or a few "you remind me of *insert YouTuber's name here*". Giving the people what they want shows that you're actually paying attention to what they're saying, and you value their opinion. This is never a bad thing.

- It's fun. It can be a lot of fun collaborating with another YouTuber. There, I said it. It's actually a blast. You're talking with somebody else who you already know is interested in the same things you are, so you already have an entire base of what you can talk about. You'll walk away with more ideas than what you came with, and you're getting creatively stimulated. It may be a little different at first, especially if you're used to working alone, but it can be a lot of fun.

Next up, we're going to talk about two things; what kind of collaborations you can do, and how to make them as smooth (and fun) as possible for you. There's a bit of a science to it.

What Kind of Collaboration?

Similar to the fact that there are about 600 types of YouTube video, there are probably about 600 types of collaboration as well. Collaboration comes in all shapes and sizes, and similar to choosing the type of YouTube videos you'll make, it really depends on what you're capable of and what your niche happens to be. But, here are some general ideas that will work for pretty much everybody.

Guest Appearances: simply just appearing on each other's channels and in each other's videos, doing a challenge or something else, is an easy way to do this. This works best if you live close to the person in your area, or if you're visiting them or vice versa.

Do a video together, and split it in half: do one video together, and divide it so one half is on your channel, and the other half is on the other channel. Just remember to include a strong call-to-action at the end, and plan who gets each half before so you can film accordingly.

Upload their video to your channel (and vice versa). If you don't live to each other, and traveling isn't an option for you right now, you have to get creative. This is a great way to bring attention to your channel and is similar to guest writing on someone's blog. Just make sure it's in your niche.

Just exchange shout-outs. Not all collaborations are videos. Some of them are just simply communicating online through Twitter or Instagram in front of your followers. Just mention each other and link to each other's pages, along with something positive or a mention of how it's helped you. You could even create a response video if you want!

Now, there are some ideas. Now, I bet your next question is; how can I make this process easy for me? Well, I've got you covered in this guide below.

Guide to Collaboration

In this part, we're going to talk about how you can make this process as easy and as simple as you can, without going overboard.

First up, find someone to collaborate with. The easiest way to collaborate with someone is to find someone who compliments you and has the same, or very similar, niche as you. The easiest way to find someone is in the search bar. Using the search filters will help tremendously. You can find people there based on their content, their subscriber base, the length of their video, and more. This may take some research and some hard work, but it also might not. It really depends. Here are some tips on what to look for;

- Someone who is around the same age. Different age groups tend to not have the same audience. There are definitely exceptions to this rule, but a 22 year old probably won't have the same opinions and audiences as a 45 year old. Of course, this doesn't apply to everyone, there are exceptions to every rule, and just finding someone whose content compliments yours should do the trick.

- Check their subscriber numbers. If you have 150 subscribers and the other person has about 250 thousand, I'm sorry, but they're not likely going to work with you. It'd be nice, and if you could swing that (like if you know the YouTuber personally), go for it. But, stick to people who have the same subscriber numbers, you'll have a much higher chance of getting a yes and actually getting things done.

- Check to be sure that they're committed. Some people get into YouTube, and they don't realize just how much of a massive undertaking it is. They just don't take it seriously. If you work with these people, you're taking on the risk that they won't take you seriously either. Only work with people who clearly have a posting schedule and are engaged on their channel. Really scope them out.

- Have your expectations set. Before you even reach out, you should know exactly what you expect of your collaboration partner, from when you're posting to how much work you want to do to how much promotion each of you will be doing on social media. Have all of these details ready, and communicate them clearly. There is no such thing as too many details and communication in collaboration, trust me.

- When you're first starting out, don't put all your eggs in one basket. Don't just prepare to collaborate with one person. If you can, reach out to multiple people. Things go wrong, and it's never a bad thing to have a few projects at once working for you.

Now that you've picked someone or a few, now it's time to reach out. Here's how you do that:

- Subscribe and comment on their videos. Bring their attention to you, but not in a spammy way. Don't bring attention to your content (yet) and actually watch their videos. Compliment it in a sincere way. You shouldn't be working with someone whose content you like anyway, so this shouldn't be too hard. Once you have started up a genuine connection, and show interest

- Make your expectations clear. Remember these expectations you laid out before you even reached out? Now is the time to put them forward. Likely, the person you're working with will have their own expectations.

Now is the time brainstorming your ideas. Bring some of your own to the table, or just meet up, either in person if you live close enough or over video chat (distance really isn't an issue when it's collaborations, so don't let yourself be limited by that). You can brainstorm together. Here's how to brainstorm productively;

- The best idea always wins. Don't get too attached personally to your idea, as it will probably change and evolve over time. That's what happens when you collaborate with someone.

You don't have full creative control, and they're going to want to get their half in too. Be open to changes or compromises.

- Create a plan. This means a plan in what gets done at what time, how often you'll be promoting each other on social media, and who will do what. Creating a schedule and sticking to it will keep everything running smoothly.

- Put something out on social media right away (if it's OK with the person you're collaborating with). Tease a collaboration on your separate social media pages, even just a tagged picture of the two of you. This will give your followers hints of what they can expect, and you could even ask them outright what content they want to see from the two of you.

- Put your best foot forward, and work hard. This could lead to more collaborations in the future, not just with this person, but any other person who sees your channel. This is all about building your relationships and showing off a bit. Don't do a mediocre job, or your collaborate partner won't want to work with you again, or anyone else. You need to impress them and their audience, some of whom may be other YouTubers you can work with, after all.

Now, all you have to do is bring together your ideas, make a few videos, and voila! You have a collaboration! Now, as you make the video and when you upload it, do the following:

- Put the links to their channel in your description box, and talk about their content in the actual video. If you're doing a video on their channel as well, be sure to link to that video as well, plus a description.

- Include an email address on where other people can reach you. When you're open to collaborations, it's important to actually tell people. This is why making it easy for people to actually contact you is an easy way to find more people to work with.

Well, I'm pretty sure that covers all about collaborations. Actually, we've covered pretty much everything content wise now. Now it's time to talk about what we all came here for; *money.*

CHAPTER 7
Money

I know what you're thinking: finally. Finally, we're at the "how to make money" part of all of this. You're finally going to be able to quit your boring day job and go right into making videos and content that you love. But, I've kind of got news for you.

It's not that easy.

Not that at any time in this book I made it out to be like it was easy. Being a YouTuber is hard work, there are long hours, and you do a lot of your work alone. For some people, that's not an ideal situation. Honestly, when YouTube is hailed as a get rich quick scheme, where all you have to do is upload a few videos and wash the cash deposit itself into your bank account, I want to roll my eyes. Nothing that is valuable is done with just a few quick videos, and any successful YouTuber, no matter how successful, will tell you that.

Before you make money, there's a lot of time, dedication, and effort you have to put it, but it's totally worth it in the end. But, it can be a long road with very little reward, so first, let's go over the rules of making money on YouTube:

1) Understand that it may take a while. And until it does happen, you have to stop focusing on money. Don't think about making money, and just think about how your videos are as a channel. Do you like them? Do you not like them? What's wrong with them? What do you like about them? How can you make them better? You need to pay attention and finetune your craft before you can make real money off of something.

2) Understand that 50 active subscribers are better over 1,000,000 inactive ones. It's rarely about the subscriber, or even view count when it comes to making money, believe it or not. So, don't get wrapped up in subscriber count, it's not nearly as important. It's only an ego boost.

3) Understand your craft, and stick to it. Once you have your niche, your strategy, and your schedule down, follow that like you would the bible. Fine tuning your craft and making sure you're putting out good content is the most important thing.

4) Understand that this is your job. This means being professional. This means that you have to treat it like you would any job that's 9 to 5. Actually, spoiler alert, a lot of YouTubers actually work much longer hours than that. But, treating this like you would any other job will really help keep your head where it's supposed to be. This also means that you can't start treating the internet like a playground; it's a workspace.

5) Understand your brand. I know that we've already talked a lot about the brand in this book, but it's important. Especially when it comes to making money. You shouldn't ever do something that if off brand, regardless of how much money you stand to make from it. You run the risk of losing a lot of your following this way, as if they see you doing things that have nothing to do with your brand, they'll assume that you're just after their money. You really don't want that.

And there you have it; these are the rules of making money off of YouTube. While these are definitely not the official, YouTube rules (we'll get into these next chapter when we're talking about monetization). They're still good to have on hand.

Now, the real question is, how long will it take for me to make money on YouTube? And the answer? Well…

How Long Will it Take Me to Make Money?

Compared to the old days, making money on YouTube is a lot more difficult than it used to be. There are a few reasons for that, but it mostly comes down to three; the competition, the number of views, and YouTube's policy.

We've already talked a lot about just how insane the competition is on YouTube, so we don't need to go over that again. But it is crazy, and that is something to keep in mind. But rather than let that deter you, let it inspire you to make sure that every piece of content you put out there is absolutely amazing and incredible. If you need to stand out in a crowd of a million people, make sure you're doing something that makes you stand out. By doing this, this is how you'll get subscribers and views.

Subscribers and views really come out of putting quality content that people are interested in out there. That's literally it. Once you have gotten enough views and subscribers, you should be able to use them to make money. This shouldn't take too long as long as you're being consistent.

Finally, YouTube's new policy. This policy, at the time of writing a book, is only about a year old and caused a huge amount of uproar when it first came out. It affected not only new YouTubers but older ones as well. What's the policy?

To monetize your channel, you need at least 1,000 subscribers and 4,000 hours of watch time, all done in the span of about 12 months. There a few reasons for this change (before it didn't matter), but one thing that seemed to really inspire it was the infamous Logan Paul video that showed him finding a dead body in the suicide forest in Japan. Other things that may have influenced it was advertisers complaining that their ads were being played on videos that put forward racist or homophobic content, something that they as a company didn't want to be associated with.

This is the big reason why it's so important to really hammer home for subscribers and views that first year. It can be a little intense and can take some getting used to, but if you want to make money with monetization, it's important. Of course, there are other ways to make money on YouTube that don't involve monetization, and we'll get into that now.

How To Make Money on YouTube

Now, there are so many different ways to make money through YouTube that you would need about 800 pages to get through all of them. There are so many cool and creative ways that people have found a way to make money online, and you really have to hand it to them. I doubt that when YouTube started off, they thought that one day there'd be people making millions every month just off of posting videos of their day to day lives. It's kind of crazy, no matter how you think about it.

But, anyway, when it comes to making money, you really just have to be creative. I can give you these options, yes, and we're going to devote a chapter to each of them, but it's up to you. In each individual chapter, we're going to get into how you can into it, the easiest ways to get into it, and more. Let's get started.

Monetization: this is the one that people generally think of when they think of a YouTuber making money off of the platform. It's also generally the one that makes people the least amount of money. Advertisers have gotten notoriously picky about what kind of content they want their videos to be on, and not only that but rates have been going down. But, that doesn't mean that it's still not an option to try out for you and that you shouldn't be doing it. In fact, it means exactly the opposite.

Affiliate Marketing: this is a way that you can take advertising directly into your own hands. You choose which products or services you speak of on your channel. It could even be your own! But, this can also erode trust with potential and current subscribers, so be sure that you never find yourself being paid to say you like something. If you're being paid to say you like something, and a subscriber goes out and buys that thing and it's not very good, the person who gets the heat will be you. Not the company that made the product, but you for suggesting it. You want to establish a level of trust with your followers, and just saying you like something for money is one of the easiest ways to lose that.

Selling: if you want to sell on YouTube, the first thing you should know is that you need to do two things; you need to be able to sell a product, and you need to do it a way that's personal and not too sales pitchy. You can either sell products that you believe in, or you can sell your own. There are plenty of YouTubers online who sell their own merchandise, some of them just simple T-shirts and mugs. This one takes a bit more investing than the other four on here, but if you can find a need for something, why not sell it?

Fan Funding: there is no limit to what project you can do, as long as you have enough money to do so. Before doing this, you usually had to go to big scale producers to convince them to give you money for projects, but now, thanks to the internet and the cameras in our phones, anyone can do this. Not only that but if your project is good enough, you can get other people to help foot the bill for you. If you can get enough people to believe in your channel and your content, using a program like Patreon or Kickstarter is a perfectly valid option.

There are, of course, plenty of ways to make money on YouTube. This is only the basic, average list and pretty much every big YouTuber out there has pretty much everything on this list.

Personally, I would recommend starting off with one or two of them, and as you get more organized and used to the process, then you move up into doing more. Don't overdo it or you just won't get anything done. Crashing and burning is not how you want to start off your YouTube career.

Which ones you choose to do is really all up to you, and what your channel is. Different channels will warrant different types of money. For example, if you're a makeup reviewing channel, affiliate marketing is probably where you'll aim. If you're doing skits on YouTube, Fan Funding is probably the way to go. It all depends on you.

So, now we're going to talk about each of these different forms of money making, and you can pick and choose which one you want to do.

CHAPTER 8
Becoming A Youtube Partner

When more and more YouTubers started pulling in thousands, or in some cases millions and billions, of views online, YouTube realized they needed to do something about it. These YouTubers were bringing people to their website, and as a result, to their advertisers. And that's when they came up with their partnership program. It was a way to make sure that the YouTubers were getting money for what they were doing, encouraging them to keep creating and posting on the platform. It's simple, and it's absolutely up to you as to whether or not you want to participate in it.

It works like this: you create and publish videos onto your channel. Your subscribers view them, and each time that someone views one of your videos and sees the ads, you get paid. For every click, you earn revenue. However, how much you earn depends on a variety of things, from the type of ad that the viewer sees or how they respond to it. For example, if a short commercial appears at the start of your video and the viewer chooses to skip it, you will not earn anything on that ad. Not only that, but even to just earn a few dollars requires thousands or tens of thousands of views every month. How does this work and how can you get into it?

These are the questions we're seeking to answer in this chapter.

Becoming a YouTube partner used to be a lot easier than it is now. In 2018, their program eligibility requirements were updated. This was mostly thanks to the fact that advertisers were complaining over their ads being shown over inappropriate videos. While any YouTuber can apply for the partnership program, but you have to meet these requirements to be accepted into it.

- Everything must be original.

- Your channel has 1,000 subscribers, 4,000 watch hours in the last 12 months, that shows it is still growing.

- A linked AdSense account (look ahead)

You can check your watch hours in the Analytics tab in the Creator's studio, so you know what is working for your channel and what isn't. When you apply, all of your channel activity is reviewed so they can be sure you meet the guidelines. This process could take a few weeks, and YouTube will let you know when it's done. If you want to check the status of your application, go to Creator's Studio - Channel - Monetization.

Whether or not somebody chooses to become a YouTube partner is optional, and it's all about what you want for your channel. Let's take a look at some of the pros and the cons of being a YouTube channel. Knowing them will help you make your decision.

Becoming A YouTube Partner: Pros and Cons

I like to start with the positive side of things first, and there are a lot of them when it comes to joining the YouTube program, so here are the pros.

Pros

1) You own your own content. When you upload to YouTube and you're not a partner, they can use your content however they like. When you're a partner, you own all the copyrights and distribution rights to ALL of their uploaded content, no exceptions. This means that you can upload on other websites, not just YouTube.

2) It does make you money. While it may not make you as much as other streams will, ad revenue will bring in some

extra cash. There are new features being added to help make you more money as well, such as different kinds of advertising.

3) It's all automated. When you become a YouTube partner, Google takes your channel and handles all of the advertising. It pairs you with advertisers, chooses what ads will appear, and tracks all of the traffic on it. Then, it will pay you accordingly, with you doing very little work. You don't have to go out looking for them.

4) You get more exposure. As a partner, YouTube wants to make sure that you're getting as many views as possible. This will put your content at the top of video searches pertaining to it, and there are no restrictions as to where your content will be delivered.

5) More page customization. As a YouTube partner, you'll be able to customize your page with colors and more. You can choose colors to match your brand.

6) More control. YouTube partners have more control over their content when compared to channels that aren't partnered.

7) Lots of other features. YouTube is constantly adding more to the program, as more and more ways to make money for the platform pop up. YouTube wants to make sure they're nurturing their relationship with their YouTubers, so they're willing to listen and want to work together. There's no telling what features they'll be adding next.

Of course, not everything is good in the world, not even in the world of YouTube. There are some not so great things about the YouTube partnership program. Let's take a look.

Cons

1) All your content must be 100% original. That, or you need the permission of the creator to use it. YouTube has a policy that if their algorithm even picks up a 2 second clip on videos that aren't yours you won't get a cent of that revenue. Everything that you post if you're a YouTube partner must be yours and yours alone, no exceptions.

2) Language and location restrictions. If you're not a resident in certain countries, you cannot become a YouTube partner. The only countries eligible are from Australia, Brazil, Canada, France, Germany, Ireland, Japan, Spain, Great Britain, New Zealand, and of course the United States. Keep in mind that if you aren't in one of these countries, it probably wouldn't be a bad idea, considering that it'll be expanding to new countries all the time. Early bird gets the worm.

3) Strict rules to follow. If there is one group that has to follow YouTube's rules more than the rest of them, it's YouTube partners. YouTube partners must remain in good standing with the website, and run the risk of suspension or even losing their channel if something happens.

It's hard to say whether or not it's worth it to become a YouTube partner. After all, it's up to you and how you want to run your channel. It also depends on the kind of channel you want to be. If you plan on publishing nothing but original content, I would say apply.

But one benefit of it is that it's totally optional. You can choose whether or not you take part in it. Of course, it does take some hard work, considering the amount of effort that goes into getting 1,000 subscribers and 4,000 viewing hours. Even so, it will still take a lot of time and hard work to earn anything substantial. Most YouTubers make only about 1 dollar for every thousand views. This varies YouTuber to YouTuber, but regardless, you're going to be earning peanuts at first. Here are where you should be putting all your focus in if getting approved for the partnership program is your goal:

1. Create content that is yours and yours alone, but also high quality. There are plenty of YouTubers out there who are at the top of their game now who claim that how they got there was through experimentation. Well, most of these YouTubers who started out when the average YouTuber was putting on bad content. This meant that viewers really didn't have many choices as to where they were going. This is not the same now, with high quality content being cranked out along with. While experimentation is good at the beginning a bit, I won't ever tell someone not to make sure that every video isn't high quality. This doesn't mean you need to know how to use the best editing programs and have the best cameras. This means do the best you can do every time that you post a video and make sure that you did the best every single time. People notice the quality and hard work, and YouTube is not an exception to that rule.

2. Stick with your niche. For the first few months/years, you're going to have to stay in your niche if you're really focused on building your subscriber base. They're going to be coming to you for a certain type of content that you promise, and if you don't deliver, they're going to be disappointed. Consistency with your niche, plus as to what time you post, will help build subscribers.

3. Engage with your audience. Remind your audience to subscribe to every single video. Remember, your audience likely actually want you to keep making content. So, they want you to make money off of it, maybe not directly. This is why programs such as Patreon work so well because people want their favorite creators to keep going. So, reply

to comments, remind them to subscribe, and ask questions, either in the videos or in the comments.

4. Follow all the strategies in this book. A lot of what you've read here is stuff that you've already read in this book. But, this is because it really is all that simple. You just need to keep following the formula. YouTube isn't an art; it's a science, and the quicker that you understand that the faster you will make money.

How To Apply For YouTube Partnership Program

Once you have gotten your 1,000 subscribers and 4,000 viewing hours, now it's time to apply for the program.

First, you're going to need an AdSense account. An AdSense account is a program run by Google. It allows people in their network to serve text, video, image, video, or other interactive ads on their websites, as long as it's a Google based content website. One of these websites is YouTube. You can choose the types of ads you want to run, where and when you want your ad to appear, and eventually, if you become big enough, advertisers will actually start bidding on your videos, similar to an auction. This means you're making more money.

To create an AdSense account, follow the following steps:

1) Go to google.com/AdSense/start.

2) Click the green sign up now button.

3) Enter the URL of your YouTube channel. Using your YouTube channel, you can then click continue in... after you enter your URL. This will go faster then.

4) From there, you can choose whether you'd like AdSense to send help. They will send you tips on performance that is

tailored to you, and a lot of beginner YouTubers (and creators online) find it very helpful.

5) Review the terms and conditions to make sure that you're not getting a surprise later.

6) Congratulations, now you have an AdSense account!

Now all you have to do is apply for the YouTube Partnership Program. After applying, this may take a few weeks, and there are no guarantees that you're going to be accepted. But no worries, you can just try again!

1) Sign into YouTube.

2) In the top right corner, select your account icon. Scroll down to the creator studio.

3) When the creator studio opens, head to the left sidebar. Select channel, then Status and features.

4) Under monetization, then click enable.

5) Follow the on-screen steps, which will guide you through the entire process.

Whether or not you choose to enter the YouTube Partnership Program, keep in mind that you probably won't be able to make all your income just from this. You probably won't even make that much, at least at first. Even the most successful YouTubers, most of their income doesn't come from this.

A few years ago, this may have been the case, but since YouTube's crackdown on who can get monetization, that's no longer what's happening. YouTube advertisers have gotten notorious about submitting complaints about where their ads appear, so that means that your videos may not even get approved. This is all based on their content.

But, there are other ways to make money on YouTube. AdSense is not your ride or die way. So let's get into some of them. Next chapter: Affiliate Marketing.

CHAPTER 9
Affiliate Marketing

The concept behind affiliate marketing is that you basically can just make money at any time throughout the day, no matter what time it is, and you can even sleep making money. Sounds nice, right?

Affiliate marketing is often used by companies to help drive up their sales and will bring you large amounts of revenue if you do it correctly. This means that both the company and the person doing the marketing wins in this situation.

While you may think that it's really hard to get into it, that's just not the case. The stats are in, and there is plenty of affiliate marketing opportunities for everyone.

- 81% of brands regularly use affiliate marketing when they're putting a new product out in the world. This number will only get higher as more and more brands become aware that this is an option. Every year, the increase in the amount of spending done by brands for affiliate marketing goes up about 10%.

- 16% of all online orders made are because of affiliate marketing, with content marketing generating three times more than more traditional methods of advertising.

We've pretty much all seen affiliate marketing. It's when a company pays someone, usually a celebrity in the olden days, and talk about how much they like the product. Every time a Kardashian posts a coupon code online, they're getting a slice of the cash generated from each of these coupon use.

The actual definition of affiliate marketing is this: the process by which an affiliate (you) earns a commission for marketing another company's, brand's, business's, or person's products. Basically, you promote the product and get paid for it. The sales are tracked using coupon codes or special links called "affiliate links" that lead you from one website to another.

Here's the step by step breakdown of the process:

1) You show an ad or link for whatever product it is on your website, talk about it in your video, you post on other social media about it, etc.

2) The customer clicks on the link.

3) Customer is sent to the store.

4) The customer makes a purchase.

5) The network takes note of the purchase.

6) The purchase is confirmed by the company/brand/business/person.

7) The transaction is credited to you.

8) You get paid your commission.

These steps may seem really complicated, but they're really not. Most of the time, you're not even doing that much work. Basically, it comes down to three separate groups:

You (the Affiliate)
The Product Creator/Seller
The Consumer

To make sure that you're successful, you need to understand the relationship between these three groups of people:

The Product Creator/Seller

This person is a business. That's it. They're looking to sell something and make money from it. It can be anything, a physical object like household cleaning supplies or a brand new cell phone, or a service, like music lessons or a course on speaking French. There isn't much you can't buy on the internet these days. The seller may not be involved in the marketing process, but they could be as well.

The Affiliate

This will be you. Your job is to promote the product and persuade your subscribers that this is a great product and they need it in their lives. You need to convince them to purchase it. You won't make any money otherwise. We'll talk more about the rules of affiliate marketing in a bit, but one of the big ones is that you don't choose products that don't fall in with your niche.

The Consumer

These are the people that you need. These are the people who will drive all of your income. You can have the best product in the world, the best deals, but if nobody buys anything, you won't make anything. So, nurturing this relationship is critical. We'll get into more of this in a bit, but it's important to remember.

Affiliate marketing is a draw because it seems to be really easy. It's quick, costs very little money, but it's also one of these things that do require some grind at the beginning of your time doing it. You may not make money for months.

To be fair, there are several ways an affiliate marketer to make money. In most cases, affiliate marketers only get paid in pay per sale. This is when you get a percentage of the money made off the product after the consumer actually makes a purchase through the affiliate marketer's strategies. This means that you actually have to get someone to buy the product before you get paid.

There are two other methods, but you'll have a hard time using them if you're just starting out. These are "pay per click" and "pay per lead".

Pay per click is simply if you can get someone to click on a link, then you get paid. You're paid based on the increase of web traffic from your link, and the more web traffic you can drum up, the more you get paid. This is obviously the most ideal one because it's a lot easier to get someone to just simply click on a link rather than actually buys something. But, offers like these are rare, unless you're a celebrity or someone with 10 million subscribers.

The third way that affiliate marketers work is pay per lead. Pay per lead is a bit more complex than the other two we've mentioned. This one is based on how far you can get a potential viewer to go. How many links can you get them to click, can you get them to enter a certain code, all of these things. You have to get someone to go onto another website to complete an act of some kind. It will depend from brand to brand, but examples include subscribing to a newsletter, downloading software, or signing a petition. It really all depends.

And that is pretty much basically what affiliate marketing is.

YouTube is the perfect place to get started affiliate marketing. There are plenty of YouTubers who take a part of it. Spend enough time on the platform and eventually, you're going to find YouTubers talking about services and products from other parts of the internet. It comes with the territory of YouTube now.

Once you have built up a large enough following, you can start finding people to work with. Let's start first by looking at how

YouTube cannot just help you get into it, but what requirements you need to look for when you do find products that you want to talk about.

The Rules of Affiliate Marketing

1) Must always fall into your niche. Why would you promote a product that you aren't sure your followers would actually be interested in? This means that if you get offered to become a marketer for a hair products company and you're a channel who focuses on health and fitness, your followers aren't following you for the tips on the latest beauty products. No. They want things like new protein powders and the most advanced workout gear available. That's what they want to see sponsoring your videos. So, if you're going to market to anyone, market to them. They're the ones who are going to be clicking. Of course, there are some niches that are so diverse they don't really have to worry about this (think comedy skits or business advice), but what they choose to market on their channel should also cater to a large audience (coffee, office supplies, etc.).

2) Always be products that you actually believe in. Too many marketers make this mistake where they choose to put their voice behind a product that they don't actually believe in. This means they don't actually use it, or they haven't even touched it, or they know that it's not a good product. This is a huge mistake, as it ruins the trust between you and your subscribers. Your monetary gain depends on their support, remember? Bonus points if you can find a company that you already love that's willing to work with you.

3) Do your homework. If it's a new brand, do your homework on it. Yes, on the surface they may match you perfectly but underneath it all. Maybe the product looks good on the surface but actually isn't that great once you have taken it

around for a few spins. Be sure to actually test out what they're selling before you sign anything, and ask for a free trial of a few days every time (at least).

4) Pay attention to new products that are coming out. Always stay on top of the new products that you may want to support. This goes hand in hand in making sure that you've also got the latest news on your own niche. If there is a company that you've worked with, or you want to work with, that's coming out with new features, you want to be aware so you can offer your services up front.

Now, to get into affiliate marketing, it's not as hard as most people think it is. People often assume that you need 100,000 subscribers to get started, but you really don't. The easiest way to get into affiliate marketing is to join an affiliate program. Don't know what that is? Keep reading.

Affiliate Marketing Programs

So, for those who don't know, affiliate marketing programs are basically just an easy way for brands looking for YouTubers and bloggers and other content creators to work with. Many YouTubers are already signed up for large affiliate marketing programs like Amazon's one (which we'll be talking about), but I have great news for you: there is no limit to how many affiliate programs that you can sign up. There are literally hundreds, and most YouTubers don't realize just how much money they could be making if they just did a little research. Don't be one of them.

Here are some of the best affiliate programs available online as of 2019. These are catered to a certain user base, and different programs will have different kinds of offers. This means that you probably won't fit with every affiliate program on this list, and it's all about what works for you. Some of them just won't have offers that are in the same niche as your channel. But, I did my best to cover all the bases. But, even if I missed it, there are plenty of other websites online. You just may have to do some digging.

Movani

If you're a channel who focuses on photography, cinematography, or anything really art or movie related, this one's for you. Their affiliate program is incredibly attractive, as they start their margins at 40% (for every purchase, you get 40% of the profit), and they're well known and raved about. Even if you're not a channel about art or photography or videography, they do have products that aren't necessarily hard to sell. There are plenty of people who are looking to break into the YouTube game themselves, and Movani's products can help them do this.

Nintendo Creators Program

Yes, gamers, your dreams have been answered. Nintendo has an affiliate program. This was created after YouTube gamers used Nintendo games on the platform. Basically, when you use Nintendo games in your videos, Nintendo receives a cut of any ads you get, and you get some of that. Pretty sweet, right? You have a choice between registering your entire channel or just a couple of videos, and you can get 60% to 70% of each cut.

PointsPrizes

An easy, basic platform, this works by you including referral links at the top of your video descriptions that are relevant to your audience. This is one of these channels that run off of traffic rather than actual purchases. All you have to direct them over to whatever website it is, and they pay much more than other affiliate programs (up to 10 times the amount). They're also not interested in changing your content.

Sigma Beauty

Hands up for all the beauty gurus! Basically, this one works by you signing up for the program, receiving a special affiliate code, and reading their instructions. Sigma would rather you use all of their brushes by name, and including all the links in your about section on your profile, as well as your description box. This seems like a lot, but it can earn you a lot of money. Especially since the amount all depends on the amount that you sell.

Amazon

The king of the internet, Amazon is usually the first program any YouTuber signs up for. It's easy, free to join, and there isn't much of a sign-up or approval process. You basically just choose whichever products you want to advertise, and you can earn up to 10% in fees. Most YouTubers choose to put up links for their camera gear or any item they're using in their videos, as they can vouch for the products without even having to outright mention it.

Shopify

This little known e-commerce platform is a treasure trove for YouTubers. How Shopify works is that you spread the word on your channel, and encourage others to sign up for it. There are reports that you can earn almost $60 for every user that signs up for your own link! Plus, there is around the clock support, with links to blogs, tutorials, and more. This will help you really understand the platform and able to adequately explain it to your audience.

Here are some other ideas on how to find brands that you want to work with:

- Follow others' examples. If there is a lot of YouTubers promoting one thing on YouTube at any time, you can bet that there is probably a brand behind it that wants more to work with. When a business first launches, they're working to get the word out there as quickly as possible. If you may be able to help with that, jump on it right away.

- Reach out yourself. Now, I'm not saying that Coca-Cola will want to work with you if you just give them a call (I mean if you can swing it, go for it). But, if there is a brand that you really enjoy, such as a local business or a course that you enjoyed, see if they're interested in working with you as business partners. They may sponsor one or two of your videos in exchange for you talking about them in the videos.

How To Start Making Money

Now that you've found a way to actually get affiliation deals, now it's time to talk about something else: how to get people to actually click on the links in the first place. Thankfully, there are some tricks to this that will make people more likely to tap it, and get you some cash.

- Know the product inside and out. You should really know exactly what the product is before you start selling it anyway, but if you can provide a demonstration on your channel, that's huge. By listing all the products features and showing your fans how to use it, it shows that you've done your research and actually care about what product you're showing your subscribers.

- Be honest. Never just be paid to say I like a product. We've gone over this before, but it's super important. This will 100% destroy the trust you've already established with your subscribers.

- Tell a story. If the product has a personal story that will resonate with your audience, share it. If you can find a product that answers a problem that you wish you had the answer to in the past that also fits your niche, that's the perfect fit for you.

81

- Be likable. This goes without saying, but to be a YouTuber you do have to be likable on some level or another. But, if you're likable to your fans and able to make them feel like a friend and relate to them, they're more likely to buy from you and help you out. This also goes for selling and fan funding as well.

- Treat it like you would sales. Anyone who is or has been in the sales industry, or the customer service industry, understands this. Sales really is a science, and only a select few people can do it for a long time. This means you have to make sure to keep smiling, always understand that some people just may not buy it, and some months will be slower than others. It's a slow process, but you'll get there.

The concept of affiliate marketing is pretty great. You basically just go to sleep and wake up with money coming in. But, it can be a long time before that starts to happen for you, and take some really hard work. But it is worth it and is a great way to make some money while talking about what you love. Seriously, you get to post 5- to 20-minute videos talking about a topic you love, and you only have to include a 2-minute pitch on a product you probably like anyway? That's a great deal.

Anyway, now it's time to talk not about selling other people's products, but selling your own. The next chapter, we're going to talk about merch, and how eventually, it could easily have a huge earning potential for your channel. Read on.

CHAPTER 10
Selling

Maybe you've got a product to sell. Maybe that's your whole reason for starting a channel, is because of that product, whatever it is. Having a product on YouTube that you believe in and want to sell is great, but if it's your own products it's even better. There are plenty of YouTubers out there who use YouTube to sell things, whether it's through affiliate marketing or their own products. While the last chapter was all about affiliate marketing, this one is going to be about the products that you actually create yourself.

Here's the thing, to really sell on YouTube, you need to have a product you can 100% get behind. If you read our chapter on affiliate marketing, you should know that you should never sell a product on your channel that you wouldn't use yourself. It reflects badly on your viewers. This goes double when it's your own products that you're selling. If you tell your followers how great this product is and it turns out to be a dud, you'll lose customers at an alarming rate and the sense of trust. People talk on the internet, remember that.

I would say that if you really want to sell on YouTube, you need to show that you know your stuff. For example, if you're trying to sell makeup, you need to show that you know everything about makeup. If you're trying to sell a course on speaking Japanese, you need to show that you can speak it fluently. If you're trying to give travel tips, you need to show yourself traveling and visiting a lot of different places. You need to be able to prove that you know your stuff without too much issue.

People will only buy from people who have succeeded in what they do. This is one of the reasons why blogging is so popular. If you're a cooking blog, and your blog is full of photos showing that you know what you're doing through the beautiful pictures of delicious meals and helpful tips on how to make someone else's life easier in the kitchen, they're more likely to buy from you. If you recommend it and you show that you know your stuff, and you're making your own products on top of that, people will buy from you.

We already talked a bit in the affiliate marketing chapter about how important it is to be likable when you're selling, but it's doubly important when it's your products. You also have to be transparent and honest. One of the most popular ways people sell things on YouTube is when they review other companies' products in an honest and transparent way. This doesn't mean they bash the product for no reason. Quite the opposite, actually. They give reviews in a fair review. This shows likeability and the fact that you are going to be transparent about your own products. You show your value up front.

Another option on selling on YouTube is to just sell merchandise having to do with your channel. Merch is a popular way to make money on YouTube, with some YouTubers literally making millions of dollars every year just on selling T-shirts. While I'm not saying you're going to make that much, you will definitely make a bit more money this way. This is especially popular and a good idea if you're a vlogger or personality YouTuber of some kind.

Merchandise Ideas

Did you know that Logan Paul made an estimated 5 million dollars just from his merchandise? No matter how much the internet hates the guy, you have to hand it to him. While Logan Paul excessively talks up his merch, you don't have to do this. Just simply add a store in your video (YouTube lets YouTube partners do this), and make a point to mention your products somewhere in your description. Even include it in your comments, if you dare.

84

Here are a ton of different ideas for merch. Even just picking up one or two of them can bring in some cold hard cash. Not only that, but a lot of these items are meant to be taken out in public, meaning that you'll get paid for someone to advertise for you. That may be a bad way to put this, but it works.

1) T-shirts: Do you have a cool slogan? A funny saying that you repeat all the time? A great logo? All of these things sound perfect on a T-shirt. Fun fact, did you know the reason why a lot of singers sell T-shirts is that it's an easy way to get the word out there? I mean, think about it, how many times have you seen a band T-shirt on someone, asked about it, and went home to look it up? Yeah, it happens.

2) Stickers. Stickers are perfect for kids. They're cheap to make, cheap to buy, and you often see children and teenagers putting them on their school supplies. This is one reason a lot of YouTubers, particularly whose content is aimed at children, invest in them and sell them. But, that doesn't mean that just because your content is aimed for adults, that means that you can't sell them. Adults love stickers too, after all!

3) Backpacks: similar to T-shirts, backpacks are another great way to get the word out while making money doing so. These are perfect for kids especially, as they use backpacks for school, so be sure that they come in a variety of sizes and colors. But you will probably have more success with children. Also, if they're high quality, that's just a bonus. Nobody likes a backpack that breaks after two months, so people will be less likely to buy from you again.

4) Tote Bags: if you're running a channel that's all about being environmentally conscious, this one's for you. More and more people are turning to use tote bags in place of plastic bags, which means that more people as investing in them.

This is a great opportunity for you whether or not your channel is based around living a green lifestyle.

5) Stationery Set: we may not write letters anymore, but people still love cute or cool looking stationary. Even just 20 sheets made up with neat looking designs will get some sellers. If you're an art channel or something along these lines, this is a perfect idea for you.

6) Subscription Box: literally any channel could do this. It's where you put together a box around your niche. For example, if you're an art channel you could do art supplies. Or if you're a movie channel you could do movie merch. Just have a mixture of items every month (or just one surprise item) that's worth about the same amount of money. Any mix of items is great.

7) Cell phone accessories: who doesn't have a cellphone in today's world? And who doesn't love decorating up their phone with little pieces of personality? Things like phone cases are a cheap and easy way for fans to support you.

8) Journal: writing may be going out of style, but cute notebooks are still very much in. Whether they're big notebooks meant for taking notes in class or a small daily planner, these do sell really well. They're also useful, so people actually have a need for them in the day to day life, making them more likely to sell.

9) Stuffed animals: again, stuffed animals are much more aimed at children than anyone else, but there are plenty of adults out there who will invest in them. Just one or two limited-time-offered stuffed animals can also be used as collectibles later on.

10) Perfumes: making a good perfume often takes a lot of time, energy, and money, so be warned this way take a while. However, there are plenty of celebrities out there who have

perfumes attached to their name, some of them not so great, some of them fabulous. Regardless, this is not for everyone.

11) Autographed items. If you're a channel that's doing a lot of hauls or you go to conventions to get things signed, selling it to people online is a great way to make some extra cash on the sign. There are people who specifically go to conventions to meet film and TV actors and writers for this specific purpose.

12) Hair ties. Small, but sweet. If your audience is largely female, this is a cheap and easy way to bring in some income.

13) Watches/Clocks: people may be using their phones to tell time now, but watches can still be a fun and funky way to spice up an outfit. Since they're mostly used as accessories, make sure that they look good.

14) Jewelry: earrings, necklaces, bracelets, or rings, all of them are a great addition to your store.

15) Makeup/Toiletry Bags: this is one of those things that is sold by a lot of makeup artists, and there aren't too many people on this planet who don't need a toiletry bag. The bigger and nicely colored, the better.

16) Socks: socks are one of these gifts that everybody hated getting at Christmas when they were kids but now, not so much. Now we all wish we had more.

17) Mugs and Travel Mugs: we all have that one friend who collects mugs like they are priceless treasures, right? I mean, I'm not the only one with that friend? Mugs are a perfect little gift for a friend, and relatively cheap to get made. You can add funny cartoons, little sayings, and more. Bonus points if you choose to get the ones that change color or pattern when hot water is added to them.

18) Slippers: everybody loves slippers, right? Perfect for lounging around the house in PJs watching YouTube videos, which is exactly what you want your subscribers to be doing. Be sure to offer them in a variety of colors and have a little fun with them. They could be classified as gifts for friends.

19) Hoodies: yet another thing that people love and an easy way to advertise. Who loses here?

20) Pins and badges: a cute thing to stick on your purse, your bag, your jacket, whatever you want. Either way, apparently pins are back, and you often see kids sewing badges onto their backpacks.

21) Lanyard/Keychains: who doesn't have keys to carry around? Even kids who have no keys love keychains. Keep them in your channel colors and keep a couple of ones with fun patterns. Keychains done in your channel logo or something else that relates to it are cute too.

22) Pillows: either a couch cushion or pillows meant for sleeping on (yes there is a difference), this can be a fun addition to your store.

23) Calendar: a calendar is a staple in many households, and many people go out to find them at the beginning of every new year. Put together a bunch of fun images and maybe some quotes from your channel, match them somewhat to the month (or not, it's your choice), and have fun!

Either way, a lot of the ways you can sell things on YouTube also apply to affiliate marketing. Make sure to follow these tips for selling:

- Mention it in your videos. Even if you're not talking about your product in that specific video, it's never a bad idea to mention the fact that yes, you do have a store in your videos.

- Put your links to your website or where they can buy the products in your description. This goes hand in hand with the last tip mentioned.

- Offer coupons. Who doesn't love a good deal? Be sure to also show the deal on other places, like you Instagram or Twitter, if you choose to. But, if it's an exclusive deal only to those who watch your video, advertise the fact that there may be a deal on another network. This will draw people to your videos.

- Show followers how to use the product. A video showing how the product works, how to use it correctly, what the packaging looks like, with a run-through of all the products features will help with sales. Bonus points if you use the product casually in your videos all the time, not just that video.

- Always be honest. It's OK to fluff up the truth a bit, but don't lie outright. Be honest about where your product is manufactured, what's in it, everything. It shows authenticity and transparency and means that more people will be likely to trust you.

Basically, now that we've got affiliate marketing and selling your own products out of the way, now it's time to talk about another form of making cash online that will work for anybody with truly great content: fan funding.

CHAPTER 11
Fan Funding

For anyone who remembers the old days of YouTube, it was considered absolutely the worst thing in the world to ask your subscribers for money. It was seen as cheap, lazy, and entitled. Well, these days have changed, and with services such as Patreon, and Kickstarter, it's only become easier for fans to help out their favorite creators online.

While there are way too many people out there who think that artists should do what they do for no cost, there are some decent people out there that realize that creators are people who need to eat as well. There are plenty of YouTubers, and other online creators such as artists and writers, who get funding through Patreon and Kickstarter so they can reach their goals and provide higher quality content.

People want more content from their favorite creators for a simple reason; they want more. They like it. They understand that it takes a lot of energy and time to make and that if they want more, the artist needs to be able to devote more time and energy to it. Let's say you're doing a movie and TV show analysis channel. Well, to do this, you have to watch the movies and TV shows, which can take hours depending on what it is, take notes, write the script, and edit the video together. This could be up to 100 hours' worth of work.

Fans know this. They know it takes time and energy. And if they want more, they're going to have to pay for it. This is where fan-funding comes in.

Fan-funding is great if your idea doesn't use 100% original material (look at things like movie reviews or music video covers), or if you just have a project that you're passionate about that just isn't going to make much money (comedy skits or other short films). There have been plenty of extremely successful short films that have raised thousands of dollars on Kickstarter, or Patreon. In A Heartbeat, an animated short film from university students, got $14,000 when they only needed $3,000.

Now, I'm not saying that you're going to get $14,000, but it can happen. People want to pay for good quality art, and these programs are a way to do it. In this chapter, we're going to go over not only all the ways that you can raise money but the different places online you can get it. We're also going to talk about how you can thank your fans when they do donate.

First, let's start off with the obvious: How To Raise Money.

How To Raise Money Online

Now, to be clear, Kickstarter and Patreon both work a little bit different. Patreon is more for people who want to donate to their favorite creators every month. Kickstarter, on the other hand, is more for one time projects. Let's say you're a short film writer who wants to go bigger. You're not satisfied with how low quality your films are and would like to buy some better equipment so you can put out higher quality. So, you'd probably go on Kickstarter. There, you pitch your idea to your fanbase, show them the link, set a goal, and hope that the money rolls in. On Patreon, it's much more of a month to month basis, with the same amount of people giving you money every month. But, it can be a one-time thing, just to be clear.

First, because it's the more popular one when it comes to YouTube, we're going to go over Patreon. Mostly because of how popular it is, and it's much more steady income than Kickstarter. Let's Roll.

Guide to Patreon

Patreon is the perfect place for monthly income from people who love to watch your content, and who want to see more of it. It could be as low as $5. Some creators have been known to pull in over a thousand dollars per month, meaning that this is a full time job for them. This is because they've done a lot of the things outlined in this list below, and if you follow these tips, you could too.

1) Build your fan base first. To really be successful at Patreon, you're going to need to have content that speaks for you already. People aren't going to invest in you unless they see you can actually do the work. This means putting in the work and the time to really connect with your fans, putting in a whole lot of effort to make sure that your videos are the best they can be, and giving people something that they want to give money to. There is no such thing as a person who just scrolls through Patreon looking for somebody to give their money to. That's a total myth. But, a person who loves a creator and wants better content does. Keep in mind that you don't need a lot of subscribers to do this. Even if you could get 50 subscribers to donate $2, that's $100 dollars!

2) Look to other Patreon examples. There is no shame in copying other people's work in this situation. Check out the other examples of what people are doing, probably some of your favorite creators. Take note of what they all have in common, and really look to see what you like and don't like. There will be potential investors who share these opinions and will donate to your campaign based on that. Patreon is still relatively new, but people are using it. Learn from their mistakes.

3) Be upfront and clear in your introductory. When you create a Patreon account, you get a Patreon clip, basically a three minute video explaining what you do. Make sure that potential Patreon supporters know exactly what they'll be getting when they donate to your fund. Be passionate and sincere in when you pitch to them, and approach it the way you would approach investors. Be passionate, direct, and sincere. Get them pumped up for your content.

4) Let your followers know what they'll be getting with goals. You can set a goal by telling your followers "if I can raise this much money, I'll do this...". Remember this; Patreon donations are literally money that comes out of the pockets of people who want certain content from you. That means communicating with them, giving the options, and more. Setting goals mean showing your viewers what they stand to gain when they donate. When you're first starting off, I would start with just one or two goals.

5) Use the reward tier system. When people donate to you, there should be some sort of reward. However, on Patreon, you can create tiers. Meaning, that the more money someone donates, the more rewards they get. These rewards can be anything, from getting access to videos of your recorded bloopers, to participating in special group discussions, to being able to get content earlier than other supporters. Higher tier rewards may not get as much attention as the $1 to $2 ones, but some people will jump at the chance to get special treatment. Do a lot of different levels, as this encourages other people to donate.

6) Promote it. Remember to tweet about your Patreon, mention it at the end of all your videos, and keep a link of it in your Instagram. Just make sure it's all over your

social media feeds, so people know to support you. Just be sure to remind your fans, so they know that they can support you. Don't just mention it once.

7) Keep it unique. Remember, the more unique your content is, the more likely it is going to go viral. It's the same thing with your Patreon account. The better the rewards, the better content you're offering, the better the Patreon trailer, the better you will do.

8) Keep shipping costs in mind. If some of your rewards are physical items (like something from your store, perhaps?), then consider the cost of shipping. You don't want to blow all the money that people have given you to create good content on sending out T-shirts and mugs. It gets even more expensive if some of your backers are from foreign countries. Keeping physical items to envelop size will help lower the costs tremendously if you really want to have a personal item.

9) Don't forget about your non-patrons. Look, the people who are donating money are amazing. They're incredible, actually. They love your content that you're offering for free so much that they're paying you to make more. But, there are probably still watchers who aren't paying. You don't know their situation. They could be young kids, people who just can't afford it, or people who aren't sold on your channel enough to pay for it just yet. Keep creating for them, and don't put all of your good content behind a paywall. Actually, I would say very little of your content should be behind a paywall; come up with creative little bonuses for your patrons rather than the content that your channel is known for.

10) Always remember to say thank you.

Good content doesn't just appear out of thin air. It really doesn't. And people who support artists and creators on Patreon understand this. But, it also takes a lot of work to make sure that people will actually support you, which is why it's so important to follow the tips outlined in this chapter.

Patreon is admittedly better for those who plan on creating content all the time. Who posts weekly. If you're not going to be one of these YouTubers (despite the fact that I would recommend that you don't), or if you want to just have a Patreon account with regular content while doing special content every once in a while, Kickstarter is another great place to go. Let's go.

Guide to Kickstarter

Now, Kickstarter is a bit more tricky. It requires a lot more planning, and because you have a limited amount of time to raise money. It's also better for if you have a special project that you've never done before coming up, something that is entirely new and fresh. So, follow these tips on how to create a successful Kickstarter Strategy.

1) Do research. When you post something to Kickstarter, you are literally competing with thousands of other projects, some that may be pretty similar to your own. While there are some crazy success stories out there where they raise double or triple the amount that they need, it probably won't be you. So, do some research. Look at the successful campaigns and see what has worked for them and what hasn't. Look under sections such as "popular" or "staff picks", as these are the best of the best. Check out the ones that are similar to your idea of the perfect campaign, and that will give you an idea of what your goals should be.

2) Know exactly what your goal is. How much do you need? What do you want to accomplish with it? Don't overextend. On Kickstarter, if you don't reach your goal, you literally get nothing, so it's better to have the most reasonable number you can muster. This is also another reason why it's important to have an audience that you can share this campaign with, as they will donate, thus bumping your campaign up a bit to get more recognition.

3) Consider rewards before you get started. Similar to Patreon, people want something in exchange for donating. Consider how much you can spend, and don't forget to consider mailing costs if necessary as well.

4) Make sure your pitch is really good. A good or bad pitch can be the difference between a successful campaign and an unsuccessful one. You're going to have to mention your goals, your rewards, and your project. You need to be specific, and I would definitely recommend creating a video. They're known to get more funding, and it shouldn't be too hard considering that you're a YouTuber, right? You want to get people excited about your upcoming project, whatever it is and show a lot of enthusiasm and passion.

5) Market, market, market. You can choose what is your deadline for when you need to get the money for it, but you do have limitations depending on the amount. Once you have gotten the project published, market it like a crazy person, whether it's on your channel or through other social media networks. You should also be encouraging your fans to bring their friends to it. You could even try pitching to other YouTubers that you know and who will support you.

6) Keep going. One of the biggest mistakes a lot of Kickstarter make is not keeping at it. This means letting your followers and friends know how it's going, updating on the progress and reminding them that it exists. Even add more rewards as time passes.

7) Patience. Just like with Patreon, some days the money will flow in smoothly, other days, not so much. You need to be creative, positive, and keep your head screwed on the right way. If it doesn't work out this time, try again in a few months. Keep spreading the word, and if your project speaks for itself, it will get there.

8) Be creative, and nothing ever goes as planned. As a YouTuber, you should be ready to try new and different things anyway. Raising money is no exception to that rule. Be ready to try a whole bunch of things you weren't ready to try before.

Remember, at the end of the day, people online, whether or not they follow you, really don't owe you anything. Your posting content on a website that is free for anyone to make an account on. They can watch your videos as much as they wish without paying a dime.

This goes without saying, but this is why you need to have a topic that you're passionate about. You won't be able to get people to care about whether or not you can make new content if you don't actually feel the same way about the content. People don't owe you anything, so you need to make them care. That's the basic rule of any fundraising. Good luck.

CHAPTER 12
Self

Being a YouTuber is hard work. It really is. There, I said it. I'm not one to really tiptoe around things. While a lot of YouTubers (and mainstream media, actually) tend to glamorize YouTubing as this easy thing to get into that requires very little work, that is far from the truth. To be a full-time YouTuber takes a lot of dedication, time and energy, and could eat up your life in a very literal sense.

The best word to describe a YouTuber's day to day life is compact. You have to know how to do so many different things, such as video editing, writing scripts, using a camera and it's gear correctly, how to appear on camera, relating to others, lighting, a thorough understanding of the internet, and more and more. It requires constant planning, sometimes months or even years in advance. You're often working 12 to 14 hour days, which can wear down on you fast.

There has been a lot of evidence that actually links YouTubers to things like depression and anxiety, and other mental health issues. This is because of how isolated they are, often working long hours at home and usually alone. This is why I included this chapter. This chapter is full of tips on how to navigate this issue, keeping yourself healthy while still putting enough time and energy into your videos that you're still making a good living.

First, we're going to go over what a typical day in the life looks for in a YouTuber.

A Day In The Life

Of course, this will differ greatly on a few things, such as the type of channel you run and what day of the week it is. This is just a basic idea of what you could be doing day to day. Now, to keep yourself sane, it's best to keep yourself on a steady schedule. This doesn't mean that you won't have days that run longer than usual. But, at least having a schedule will at least give you a goal to get going.

Start of the day:

Wake up, morning routine; breakfast, shower, get dressed, etc.
Scriptwriting, and/or Research
Preparing for filming (learning lines, researching locations, setting up collaborations)
Spending time on social media networks, replying to comments on your channel, checking the analytics
Get ready for filming (get in touch with whoever you're collaborating if you are, confirm locations, pull together your camera gear)
Meet up with your team (if you have one)
Begin Filming; promote new content and behind the scene photos on your social media channels during this period
Film and/or record all your content
Clean up
Edit; keep promoting as you're doing it
Check your social media accounts again; reply to comments
Edit again; watch through the video twice
Go to bed; don't post the video until you've gotten a good night sleep and you've taken some time away from it. It will help you catch mistakes that you didn't the night before.

Yeah. There are some YouTubers who do this all in one day, and many of them do it alone. You really don't want to get sucked into this, especially if you're working solo. I get it, you love your job, and you want to be successful at this, but if you really want to be successful, you'll understand that this isn't the answer. While grinding and consistency are important (we'll also be talking about that in this next chapter), it's also important to take care of yourself. Here are a few ways you can do that:

- Get human contact. If you're working alone, and even if you're one of these people who claim to dislike hanging out with other people, getting human contact from friends and family occasionally will help you out. It will keep you from getting too sucked into the world of YouTube. Even doing collaborations with people in person will dramatically help your mental health, as you're still working with other people. Just be sure that the friendship isn't just for the views, and is actually genuine.

- Eat healthily and get enough sleep. Taking care of yourself is essential if you really want to succeed in this career. Yes, you can eat cereal all day and give yourself only 6 hours of sleep every night, but if you want to be at your optimal level, a nutritious diet and 8 hours of sleep every night will really serve you better.

- Get fresh air. Get off that screen occasionally. One method a lot of YouTubers use is to take a walk around the block every 2 hours. This gets their brain working again and gives them some breathing room. There are other ways to do this, but just giving yourself a break is really important.

- Give yourself vacations and breaks. Once you've transitioned into being a full-time YouTuber, it's OK to take a few weeks out of the year where you literally disappear. Why not? Just give your subscribers some notice and keep writing down ideas for videos when you get them. This doesn't mean disappear for 5 weeks at a time. Bonus points if you can schedule your videos in advance so your followers are still getting new content while you're just laying on a beach somewhere.

- Don't be afraid to hire someone. Once you've reached a point where you're making a substantial amount of money, putting the editing work on someone else isn't a bad idea if editing isn't your strong suit. Or, if you want someone to do the camera work, or help you with writing. Whatever you feel you need help with. Of course, if you're not financially prepared to do this, this may not be for you.

- Don't get too caught up in views and subscribers. Views and subscribers are great. Actually, they're basically how you're going to be making your money. But they're not everything. It can be easy to get too obsessed with accomplishing the next batch of subscribers, the next batch of money makers. Instead of getting too caught up in the number of subscribers, choose to really focus on the content you're making. You're determined to make amazing content, not get a ton of subscribers. That should be your focus. And the most important part is that your value is not determined by how many followers you have. At the end of the day, they're just imaginary internet points. Literally.

Just remember to keep yourself healthy. Make time for yourself and your friends. Don't get caught in the trap of just obsessing over the next video. It's not going to serve you, or your content, well in the future.

The Importance of Grind and Consistency

So what's grind and what's consistency?

Grind is the determination you need. It's the spirit that you need to be able to get through every day, no matter how hard it is. It's what you need to wake up, put in your absolute hardest work, and go to bed every night to get up and do it all over again, even if things don't pay off for you. And with YouTube, they may not, at least not for a while. This is why it's important to keep trying and keep going. Yes, we'd all love it if our videos went viral overnight and made us a million dollars, but this probably won't happen. It can take years. This is why you need to grind.

Consistency, on the other hand, is keeping to the schedule. It's waking up every day and getting things checked off your checklist. It's about showing up for yourself because you know that if you're consistent with all these little steps, they'll add up to a huge step. And eventually, all you'll be taking are big steps, because of all these little steps you took at the beginning. Consistency is keeping yourself on track. It's about holding yourself up to the standards you've set for yourself, and nailing them every time. This section is all about how you can meet these standards on your YouTube channel and keeping yourself inspired, all with grinding constantly day in and day out.

1) Figure out your end goal with your channel. And by "end goal" I mean ask yourself; what would your perfect channel look like? You need to know exactly what you're aiming for, and where you want to get. You can do this really creatively, even making a vlog of yourself talking to yourself that you can watch back every few months. Be as descriptive as you can, and every time you find yourself getting unmotivated, watch that video. You could also write a letter to yourself or an essay. The choice is yours.

2) Break up everything into tiny steps. One of the best tips I got for getting things done, especially more self-done things like a YouTube channel, is to break up every single task into smaller tasks possible. Small milestones keep you motivated, as you see things adding up quickly as you get closer to your goal. Want to get your first 100 subscribers? Write down exactly what you need to do to accomplish that goal into tiny steps.

3) Understand why you're doing this. Why do you want to be a YouTuber? Do you want to spend all day talking about what you love? Do you want to communicate with people who love the same things you do? Do you want financial

freedom? I would avoid being motivated by money alone, as it can get tedious after a while. This is why it's important to do a channel that you're going to want to wake up and think about every day.

4) Make friends with other YouTubers. One of the most valuable lessons I ever learned was "keep the company you want to be". That means, hang out with people you admire and want to be like, ones who will keep you inspired and grinding. They'll keep you going and inspired, and doing collaborations with them is a fun way to be held accountable for your actions. They'll be expecting new content from you, just as you expect content from them.

All in all, the most important thing to remember about being a YouTuber and hanging out online is remembering that it's a job and also remembering to give yourself a break. It's a business first and foremost and should be treated like one.

This means that it's not just about waking up at 2, spending an hour or so filming, then slapping together a video that lasts about 5 minutes. It's about carefully planning out your day and being motivated to get things done. It takes a lot of thick skin too, dealing with trolls on social media, which are running rampant.

I wish everyone luck in this career. But I also want them to be realistic. The best advice I can leave you with is this:

Don't. Focus. On. The. Money.

Focus on the content. Focus on making content that you want to make, that you want to see more of. Don't get trapped in this cycle of being worried about how many subscribers you're getting and obsessively refreshing your page.

Make the content you love, and you really can't go wrong. The money will follow, just as long as you work hard and are consistent. I wish you all the luck in the world.

CONCLUSION

Thank you so much for making it through to the end of this book. I hope it was informative and able to provide you with all of the tools you need for your making money on YouTube journey.

The next step is to start trying some of these techniques and find out what works best for you. Testing out what you can do is how you get things done and how you figure out what will work for you. It will take a lot of that at first, but eventually, you'll find a way.

Lastly, if you enjoyed this book I ask that you please take the time to rate it on Amazon. Your honest review would be greatly appreciated. Thank you!

DESCRIPTION

So, you want to make money on YouTube?

When someone makes this decision to finally take control of their income and turn to this great platform, the next feeling is almost always panic. Then it's defeat. Why? Because most people just don't know how to make money on YouTube anymore. It's not like the old days where people would test out and experiment until finally, they'd stumble across it.

Nowadays, there is so much competition on YouTube that it's just better to get out ahead and have the information needed on hand. And that's where this book comes in. In this book, we're going to teach you exactly how you can make money on YouTube.

It's really easy to fall into the trap of just doing whatever. But this is not going to be how you make money. The lessons in this book include:

- A look into the history of YouTube, and the kind of person you need to be to be a YouTuber

- How to grow your subscriber base (and keep them)

- An in-depth explanation of a niche and how to find yours

- 4 different ways of bringing in income for your channel, including fan funding, affiliate marketing, and monetization

- A guide to the YouTube Partnership Program that nearly every big YouTuber is a part of

- How to get started with affiliate marketing and ideas how on how to incorporate it seamlessly into your channel

- How to start a Patreon Campaign

- How to get comfortable on YouTube with a look into what your day to day life will look like

- Why quality over quantity is so, so important in today's YouTube world

Keeping yourself informed is the first step to making a successful YouTube channel, and this book is going to take you through every step. It's a long road ahead, so you may as well have all the information that you're going to need. Actually, no, you should have all the information you need, hands down.

This book is the perfect guide for that first few months (or years) that it takes to establish your YouTube channel and start making money. These steps are easy to follow, and everything has been broken down as much as you can. Now, pick this book up, follow these steps, and watch the cash start to roll in!

CPSIA information can be obtained
at www.ICGtesting.com
Printed in the USA
LVHW010053281222
735839LV00003B/243

9 781955 617413